WHAT MORE CAN GOD SAY?

WHAT MORE CAN GOD SAY?

A Fresh Look at Hebrews

Ray C. Stedman

A Division of G/L Publications, Glendale, California, U.S.A.

The Scripture quotations in this publication are from the *Revised Standard Version,* copyrighted 1946 and 1952 by the Division of Christian Education of the NCCC in the U.S.A., and used by permission.
Others are:
[1]*King James Version*
[2]*The New Testament in Modern English,* copyright J. B. Phillips 1958. Used by permission of the Macmillan Company.

Second Printing, 1975
Third Printing, 1976
Fourth Printing, 1976

Published by
Regal Books Division, G/L Publications
Glendale, California, U.S.A.

Library of Congress Catalog Card No. 74-176002
ISBN 0-8307-0457-4

contents

A teaching and discussion guide for individual or group study with this book is available in a G/L Teaching Kit from your church supplier.

1

the final word

Some of us were gathered in a home discussing the state of affairs of the world. We commented on the fears, the tensions, the sense of futility that we find in so many circles these days. Earlier someone had read the eighth chapter of Paul's letter to the Romans, where he speaks of the whole creation groaning and travailing together in bondage, and futility stamped upon all things. In our discussion the question arose: What can we do about this? As Christians we know the answer to the world's problems, but how can we make the world believe the answer?

Among us was a young Christian who seemed considerably troubled by our discussion. With a deeply concerned look on his face, he said, "Why is this? Why doesn't the world believe what we have to say?" Then he added, "I think it's because so many Christians don't act like they believe it themselves."

Then he asked the logical but thorny question: "How can we make Christians believe what they believe?"

That is the very theme of the book of Hebrews! How to make Christians believe–how to make Christians act like Christians. This is what the world is waiting to see and what the epistle was written to produce. It is addressed to a group of Jewish Christians who had begun to drift, to lose their faith. They had lost all awareness of the relevance of their faith to the daily affairs of life. They had begun to drift into outward formal religious performance while they lost the inner reality. Doubts were creeping into their hearts from some of the humanistic philosophies that abounded in the world of their day, as they abound in the world of our day. Some of them were about to abandon their faith in Christ, not because they were attracted again by Jewish ritual and ceremony, but because of persecution and pressure. They felt that it was not worthwhile, that they were losing too much; and that it was possible, just possible, that they had been deceived and the message of Christ was not true after all.

No one knows exactly where these Christians lived. Some feel this letter was written to Hebrew Christians living in the city of Rome. Others believe it was written to the most Jewish city on earth in that day, Jerusalem. That is my own personal conviction. If anyone wished to influence the world of Jewish Christians, surely that would be the place to start. No one knows for certain who wrote the letter, either. In the *King James Version* it says, "The Epistle of Paul the Apostle to the Hebrews." It was a favorite jest in seminary to ask, "Who wrote the epistle of

Paul to the Hebrews?" No one knows for sure.

If you read this letter in English you are almost sure that Paul wrote it, since so many of the thoughts are obviously Pauline. But if you read it in Greek you are equally certain that Paul did not write it, for the language used is far different from that in Paul's letters. There have been a great many guesses throughout the centuries, including Luke, Silas, Peter, Apollos (the silver-tongued orator of the first century), Barnabas, and even Aquila and Priscilla. Some have felt that Priscilla wrote it; if so, this would be the only letter of the New Testament written by a woman. It is my own conviction that the apostle Paul wrote it in Hebrew while he was in prison those two years in Caesarea, after his visit to Jerusalem; that it was translated by Luke into Greek; and that Luke's Greek translation is the copy that has come down to us today.

Whoever the writer is, he sees one thing very clearly: that Jesus Christ is the total answer to every human need. No book of the New Testament focuses upon Christ like the book of Hebrews does. It is the clearest and most systematic presentation of the availability and adequacy of Jesus Christ in the whole of the Bible. It presents Christianity as the perfect and final religion, simply because the incomparable person and work of Jesus Christ permits men free and unrestricted access to God. In every age that is man's desperate need. There is no hunger like God-hunger.

We shall ignore chapter divisions as we go through this book. The first section covers all of chapter one and the first four verses of chapter two. We shall move quite rapidly through this epistle, for it is easy to become bogged down and to miss much of the thrust of the wonderful argument. We must move fast enough to see where the writer is going.

The argument of this first section is very simple. Somewhat bluntly and immediately, the writer declares that God has spoken to man in Jesus Christ. This is the theme of the epistle. The very nature of that word indicates that Christ is a stronger word than that which came through the prophets; He also has a greater name than that of the angels; and He Himself is a surer word to man than the law. With that as our program, let us look at the epistle.

In many and various ways God spoke of old to our fathers by the prophets; but in these last days he has spoken to us by a Son, whom he appointed the heir of all things, through whom also he created the world. He reflects the glory of God and bears the very stamp of his nature, upholding the universe by his word of power.
(Heb. 1:1-3).

In those three short verses we have four amazing themes. First that the word which now comes to us in Jesus Christ, both by what He said and by what He was, is a stronger and more inclusive word than God ever spoke through the prophets. When you read the Old Testament you are reading the Word of God. The voice of God is heard through various forms and circumstances. Open the book of Genesis and read the simple, majestic tale of creation and the flood. Then follows the straightforward narrative of the patriarchs, Abraham, Isaac and Jacob; then the thunderings of the law, the sweet singing of the Psalmist, the exalted beauty of the prophets, the homespun wisdom of the Proverbs, the delicate tenderness of the Song of Solomon, and the marvelous mysteries of the prophetic writings, as Ezekiel and Daniel. All of it is of God, but all of it is incomplete. It never brings us to ultimates and absolutes.

But when you open the pages of the New Testament and read the fourfold picture of Jesus Christ, you find that the Old merges into one voice, the voice of the Son. The syllables and phrases in which God spoke in the Old Testament are merged into one complete discourse in Jesus Christ. God's word to man has been fully uttered in the Son. There is nothing left to be said. Jesus Christ is God's final word to man. The word through the Son is greater than that through the prophets because it includes and surpasses theirs.

It is also greater because the Son forms the boundaries of history. The writer says, *Whom he appointed the heir of all things, through whom also he created the world.* In that phrase, *the heir of all things,* he is looking on into the future as far as the eye of man can see.

A teen-age boy once sat in my study with a very worried expression on his face. We talked about various things in his life, but finally he said, "I want to ask you a question."

I said, "Go ahead."

He said, "Where is it all coming to, anyway? What is happening in the world? Where is all this tremendous stirring and tumult going to end?"

I told him it would end exactly as the Bible predicted it would end. The prophetic pattern woven into the revelation of God has already been fulfilled to the very letter, as far as we have gone in history. Jesus Himself, in Matthew 24, Luke 21, and Mark 13, those great prophetic passages, indicated plainly what the end would be. He Himself is the terminating point of history. All things will end in Him. This is Paul's argument in the letter to the Ephesians, that all the events of the ages shall find their fulfillment and meaning in Jesus Christ.

Christ stands at the end of the future as He is also at the beginning of the past, for He is the Creator of the worlds. All things came from His hands; He is the originator of all the processes of life; nothing began or exists but what began or existed in Him. Jesus made this claim Himself to the astonishment of the Jews. He said, *Before Abraham was, I am* (John 8:58).

Further, His word has greater power than the prophets' because He sustains the universe. We read, *He reflects the glory of God and bears the very stamp of his nature, upholding the universe by his word of power.* In the hills behind Stanford University is a linear accelerator, some two miles long, a gigantic instrument. What is it for? Scientists hope it will prove to be a great lever by which they can pry the lid off the secrets that lie behind matter. They are trying to find what makes the universe "tick," what holds it together.

As man probes deeper into the secrets of the universe around him he discovers more and more that he is confronting the mystery of an untouchable, unweighable, unseeable force; that he stands face to face with pure force. What is that force? Scientists never name it, in fact they cannot name it, but the Scripture does. The Scripture says that force is Jesus Christ, that He holds everything in place, whether it be large or small. The reason we can sit, stand or walk, and not be hurled off into space though our earth is whirling at a furious rate, is simply because He sustains the universe. He is the secret behind everything that exists.

More than that, in the final statement here, His word comes with superior force because He redeems man and nature.

When he had made purification for sins, he sat down at the right hand of the Majesty on high.
(Heb. 1:3).

I stated earlier that we all feel the futility which is stamped upon everything today. Why is it that nothing ever completely satisfies? If we can but get certain things we think we will be happy, but once we get them we soon lose all interest in them. Why is this?

We do not believe that the world was intended to be this way, and the Scriptures confirm this. They reveal the fact that the world in which we live is a world in desperate need of redemption. It needs to be bought back out of uselessness and restored to its proper condition as it was originally intended to be. All this is included in the great statement, *When he had made purification for sins.* When He had come to grips with the thing that is destroying human life and making this universe such an unpleasant place in which to live; when He had dealt with it fully, He took His place beside the Majesty on high. That is why His word is greater than that of the prophets.

In the next section the writer moves on immediately to compare Jesus with the angels. The ancient world made a great deal of angels. They worshiped them in many of the ancient religious rites. Angels are the demigods of the Roman and Greek pantheon. Therefore, this letter was written to people who had a particular interest in angels. The writer deals with this very rapidly, but very thoroughly. This subject may not interest us as much today as it did then, but it is still a tremendous revelation of the person of Christ. The Lord Jesus, says the writer, has a greater name than the angels, first, because of His relationship,

> . . . *having become as much superior to angels as the name he has obtained is more excellent than theirs. For to what angel did God ever say, "Thou art my Son, today I have begotten thee"?*
> (Heb. 1:4,5).

The contrast is between a Son and a servant. Angels are servants but Christ is the Son. I once visited a ranch as the guest of the hired man on that ranch. When we came onto the property we had to drive around the big house and go to the bunkhouse in the rear. I stayed with him there in the bunkhouse and never once got into the big house with him. There were some beautiful sorrel horses in the pasture and I suggested we take a ride. He said, "Oh, no, I'm not permitted to ride those horses." So we had to ride some mangy fleabags out to the pasture. A few weeks later I became acquainted with the son of the household, and he invited me out to the ranch. When I went out with him it was entirely different. We went right into the big house and he took over as all teen-agers do. After a sumptuous meal we went out and rode the sorrel horses all over the range. What a wonderful time we had.

That is the difference between a son and a servant, and that is the difference between Christ and any angel. He is greater because of His relationship, the fact that He is a Son. Blood is always thicker than water. As C. S. Lewis points out, what we make with our hands is always something different from us, but what we beget with our bodies is always the dearest thing in the world to us because it is part of us. Thus, the angels were made; the Son begotten. What we beget has the same nature we have; what we make is always different. The angels, being made, cannot have the same relationship as the Son, who was begotten.

Here is the final answer to the cults. Jehovah's Witnesses teach that Jesus Christ was nothing more than an angel, the highest created angel. They identify Him with Michael, the Archangel. But this passage in Hebrews utterly demolishes that theory, for Christ is a Son and not an angel. To what angel did God ever say, *Thou art my Son*?

Second, Christ is greater than the angels by the demonstration of worship.

And again, when he brings the first-born into the

world, he says, "Let all God's angels worship him."
(Heb. 1:6).

We only worship that which is superior to us. The worship of the angels at Bethlehem is testimony to the deity of the babe in the manger. John Bunyan said, "If Jesus Christ be not God, then heaven will be filled with idolators." For in Revelation and Daniel, those books that give us a glimpse into the heavenly realms, we see ten thousand times ten thousand and thousands of thousands of angels engaged in worshiping the Son. So He is seen to be greater than angels by the demonstration of worship.

Third, His superiority is evidenced by the demonstration of authority. This section begins and ends with a word about the angels, while in between is the contrast of the position of the Son.

Of the angels he says, 'Who makes his angels winds, and his servants flames of fire'
(Heb. 1:7).

What are angels? Servants and ministers, depicted by wind and fire. In our daily life wind and fire are more than man can handle, for they frequently get out of bounds. Yet they are made to be servants of men. These symbolize the angels, superior in being to men, yet servants of men. The quotation concerning angels is from Psalm 104. Then the writer uses part of Psalm 45 to show how the Son is contrasted to the angels.

But of the Son he says, "Thy throne, O God, is for

ever and ever, the righteous scepter is the scepter of thy kingdom. Thou hast loved righteousness and hated lawlessness; therefore God, thy God, has anointed thee with the oil of gladness beyond thy comrades."
(Heb. 1:8,9).

The Son is the originator of all things. Behind all material things lies the thought and intent of the heart, and the Psalmist says of the Son, *Thy throne, O God, is for ever and ever; . . . Thou hast loved . . . and hated*[1] (Ps. 45:6,7). What God loves and hates is the motivation for what takes place within the universe. No angel can make this claim.

Again the writer moves to another quotation, this time from Psalm 102.

And, "Thou, Lord, didst found the earth in the beginning, and the heavens are the work of thy hands; they will perish, but thou remainest; they will all grow old like a garment, like a mantle thou wilt roll them up, and they will be changed. But thou art the same, and thy years will never end."
(Heb. 1:10-12).

Christ is not only the originator but the sustainer of the universe, the one behind all things, eternally keeping it going until at last it runs down. Notice a very interesting thing here, you scientists among us. There is here described very plainly what has been called "the second law of thermodynamics," the degenerative faculty in the universe. All things will grow old like a garment, but not the one who made them and who keeps them, the Son of God.

The third argument in this contrast with the angels is taken from Psalm 110.

But to what angel has he ever said, "Sit at my right hand, till I make thy enemies a stool for thy feet"? (Heb. 1:13).

Again, here is the One who waits at the end of history, the termination point of all events, the One for whom all things exist and toward whom all things are moving, the heir of all things. All things find their purpose and meaning only as they relate to Him.

The writer of Hebrews comes back to the angels again in verse 14.

Are they not all ministering spirits sent forth to serve, for the sake of those who are to obtain salvation? (Heb. 1:14).

Again, what are angels? Servants! But the Son *is* God!

Christ is not only a stronger word than the prophets, and has a higher name than the angels, but He is a surer word than the law:

Therefore we must pay the closer attention to what we have heard, lest we drift away from it. For if the message declared by angels was valid and every transgression or disobedience received a just retribution, how shall we escape if we neglect such a great salvation? It was declared at first by the Lord, and it was attested to us by those who heard him, while God also bore witness by signs and wonders and various miracles and

by gifts of the Holy Spirit distributed according to his own will.
(Heb. 2:1-4).

His conclusion is: We need to pay attention!

This convinces me that the writer of this letter, whoever he was, was a preacher. There is nothing more heartbreaking than preaching to people week after week and to see certain ones constantly exposed to truth that you know could change their lives, set them free, transform their very existence and bring them out into a realm of experience they hardly believe existed; you know this, and yet you see them, week after week, lose the whole effect of the message simply because they do not pay attention. This is why Jesus said again and again to the people of His day, *He who has ears to hear, let him hear* (Matt. 11:15). It is not too often we are able to hear truths like these; truths that go to the heart of life. But he that has ears to hear, let him hear.

There are two reasons why this message is particularly valid. First, it is valid by comparison with the law. If the word spoken by angels, the law of Moses, had validity, and those to whom it was given found that it was absolutely true in experience, then this message also is true. If angels could give a word like that, how much more should we value the word that comes by the Son?

The confirmation of this was the testimony of Israel's history. Here is a race of people, the Jews, to whom the law was particularly given. They were told that if they would obey it they would be blessed; if they disregarded it, they would be cursed. There is no people on the face of the earth who show a more consistent pattern of cause and effect than this people. Wherever they have gone, in obedience there has been blessing; in disobedience there has been cursing. If the law had that effect, a law spoken by angels, how much more shall the words spoken by the Son have effect?

The second confirmation that this message is valid is the form of its communication to us. It was spoken, first of all, by the Lord! That is a most impressive argument. What Jesus Christ has to say is the most authoritative word the world has ever heard. This message did not originate with the apostles, it did not come to us by means of prophets, it came through the Lord Himself; He spoke it.

Furthermore, the message was confirmed by eyewitnesses. This is an unimpeachable argument. Any court in the land will accept evidence if it is confirmed by enough eyewitnesses. Here is the evidence of Christianity confirmed to us by numerous eyewitnesses who were there and who wrote what they saw and heard and did.

And the message was attested by signs sent from God Himself, by wonders and miracles and gifts of the Holy Spirit, distributed according to His own will. It still is attested this way. How can we explain the gifts that develop among Christian people, the ability to do certain things, except as we recognize the Spirit of God at work in our midst? What an impelling argument this is!

It all focuses down to one question which the writer leaves hanging in the air: How shall we escape if we neglect such a great salvation? That is not a threat, it is simply a question. It is addressed both to the Christian and to the non-Christian. To the non-Christian it says, Where are you going to go? How will you get out of God's universe? How can you escape the inevitable? Indeed, why seek to avoid that which is unavoidable: a confrontation with the One who is behind all things? How can you escape, and why attempt to do so? Especially when His purpose is not to curse but to bless? How can you find deliverance by any other route, by any other path, or by any other channel, if it does not involve the One who is behind all things?

To the Christian, the writer is saying it is not enough that we know Jesus Christ: We must use the resources we have in Him. We can lose so much, even knowing Him, unless there is a day-by-day walk with Him. We lose peace and freedom and joy and achievement. We are subjected to temptation, frustration, bewilderment, bafflement and barrenness without Him. And if we do not go on as Christians, if we do not grow, a serious question is raised: Have we ever really begun the Christian life? Or is this but a self-deceptive fraud, attempted in order to meet outward standards but without any inward change in the heart? He leaves the question hanging in the air, haunting, unavoidable. And that is where we shall leave it. How shall we escape if we neglect such a great salvation? Answer that in the loneliness of your own heart.

"Our Father, the truth You have set before us is not one to trifle with. We are dealing with the very secrets of life, the very basis of the universe. The claims of the Lord Jesus are incomparable; they can never be surpassed. We pray, therefore, that we may face up to this and realize that there is no way of working out the problems of human life except as we work them out in fellowship with Him. As we go on in this letter we ask to see this even more clearly, and may hearts right now open their doors to Thee. Lord Jesus, You are the One who is the secret of human life and behind all the mysteries of the universe. May You enter our lives in grace and begin to reign.

We pray in Your name,
Amen."

2

the true man

Hebrews is all about Christ. The introduction declares that Christ is God's final word to man. There is nothing more to be said, there is nothing that can be added after what Jesus Christ has said and done. And it is utterly foolish to ignore this word, the writer says, because we cannot exist without Christ. It is basic dishonesty to pretend we can. We are not independent of God, as we sometimes foolishly imagine. We are not even independent of each other. We need one another and we need God, desperately, every moment of life. Therefore, if Christ be God, as this letter so clearly claims, He is the inevitable One, and it is foolish to ignore Him.

Now we look at a section where Christ in His humanity is set before us as our mediator before God. When man is in trouble he craves a mediator. Some years ago I was involved in a rather minor automobile accident. In my view it was entirely the other driver's fault, but apparently he did not feel the same way, because he sued me for damages. This was the first time I was ever sued, and I confess I was a bit bothered by it. But, I was comforted by the thought that this damage suit did not constitute any real threat since I had a mediator–the insurance company! I turned it all over to them and they handled the matter.

Thus, when we feel that God wants to say something to us we look around for a mediator to stand in between. The ancient world looked to angels for this service. Angels were the demigods of the Roman and Greek pantheon. But the writer of Hebrews will argue that angels will never do as mediators. The reason is simple: No angel has ever been a man; no angel has ever stood where we stand. But Jesus, the Son, has! Just how fully He has become man, we shall see in this passage. All the value of His life arises out of what we may call "the identification of incarnation."

There is an intriguing pattern developed in Hebrews 2:5-18 that I should like to indicate. Four times in this passage we are led along the course of our Lord's earthly ministry, viewing it from four different points of view. At the end of each trip we come up against the bloody cross. God has planted the cross in this passage four different times to indicate that whatever value there may be in the life of our Lord Jesus, it is made available to us by means of His death. He came to live in order that He might die. In the holy anguish of the cross, He poured forth His life in order that we may have it. The four insights of this passage accord very remarkably with the four

Gospels, Matthew, Mark, Luke and John. Here are the Gospels in miniature. They are not in the same order as the Gospels and it may add interest to this message for you to seek to identify which Gospel is indicated.

Now let us look at the first of four mighty reasons why Jesus Christ became a man.

For it was not to angels that God subjected the world to come, of which we are speaking. It has been testified somewhere, "What is man that thou art mindful of him, or the son of man, that thou carest for him? Thou didst make him for a little while lower than the angels, thou hast crowned him with glory and honor, putting everything in subjection under his feet." Now in putting everything in subjection to him, he left nothing outside his control. As it is, we do not yet see everything in subjection to him. But we see Jesus, who for a little while was made lower than the angels, crowned with glory and honor because of the suffering of death, so that by the grace of God he might taste death for every one.
(Heb. 2:5-9).

This section declares that Jesus Christ became a man **in order to recapture our lost destiny.** No angel could take Christ's place, for God had never given the right to govern the universe to angels but to men. The writer substantiates that with a quotation from the well-known Eighth Psalm, where David cries, *What is man that thou art mindful of him . . . ?* He is out beneath the stars on some soft oriental night, looking up into the majesty of the heavens and feeling his own insignificance. He asks, "Where is man's place in this universe?" and by the Spirit he answers his own question. *Thou didst make him for a little while lower than the angels, thou hast crowned him with glory and honor, putting everything in subjection under his feet.*

The writer insists that when David says "all things," he means all things, everything. For he adds, *Now in putting everything in subjection to him, he left nothing outside his control.* Here is man's intended destiny, his authorized dominion. Man was made to be king over all God's universe. Surely this passage includes far more than the earth. It envisions the created universe of God as far as man has ever been able to discover it, in all the illimitable reaches of space and whatever lies beyond that. All this is to be put under man's dominion. It is a vast and tremendous vision.

But man's authority was derived authority. Man himself was to be subject to the God who indwelt him. He was to be the means by which the invisible God became visible to His creatures. He was to be the manifestation of God's own life which dwelt in the royal residence of his human spirit. As long as man was subject to the dominion of God within him, he would be able to exercise dominion over all the universe around. Only when man accepted dominion could he exercise dominion.

The writer further points out that man was made lower than the angels for a limited time to learn what the exercise of that dominion meant. He was given a limited domain: this earth, this tiny planet whirling its way through the great galaxy to which we belong, amid all the billions of galaxies of space! And he was also given a limited physical body so that within that limited area man should learn the principles by which his dominion could be exercised throughout the universe. This limitation is described as being *lower than the angels.*

But the passage goes on to describe man's present state of futility. *As it is, we do not yet see everything in subjection to him.* There is the whole story of human history in a nutshell. How visibly true this is: we do not yet see everything in subjection to him. Man attempts to exercise his dominion but he no longer can do so adequately. He has never forgotten the position God gave him, for throughout the history of the race there is a continual restatement of the dreams of man for dominion over the earth and the universe. This is why we cannot keep off the highest mountain. We have to get up there, though we have not lost a thing up there and we know when we get there we will only see what the bear saw: the other side of the mountain. But we have to be there. We have to explore the depths of the sea. We have to get out into space. Why? Because it is there.

Man consistently manifests a remarkable racial memory, a vestigial recollection of what God told him to do. The trouble is that when he tries to accomplish this now he creates a highly explosive and dangerous situation, for his ability to exercise dominion is no longer there. Things get out of balance. This is why we are confronted with an increasingly serious situation in our day when our attempt to control insects by pesticides and other poisons creates an imbalance that threatens serious results. The history of man is one of continually precipitating a crisis by attempting to exercise dominion.

If we go back into recorded history to the earliest writings of men, the most ancient of history, we find that men were wrestling with the same moral problems then that we are wrestling with today. We have made wonderful advances in technology, but have made absolutely zero progress when it comes to moral relationships. Somewhere man has lost his relationship with God. The fall of man is the only adequate explanation of this. Since then the universe is stamped with futility. Everything man does is a dead-end street; he is utterly unable to carry things through to a successful conclusion. Even in the individual life this is true. How many have realized the dreams and ideals they began with? Who can say, "I have done all that I wanted to do; I have been all that I wanted to be." Paul in Romans puts it, *The creation was subjected to futility* (Rom. 8:20).

But, the writer of Hebrews says, *we see Jesus!* This is man's one hope. With the eye of faith we see Jesus already crowned and reigning over the universe, the man Jesus fulfilling man's lost destiny. In the last book of the Bible there is a scene where John beholds the One seated upon the throne of the universe while ten thousand times ten thousands and thousands of angels are crying out in unending, undying worship before the throne. The call goes out to find one who is able to open the little book with seven seals which is the title deed to earth, the right to run the earth. A search is made through the length and breadth of human history for someone wise enough, strong enough, and compassionate enough to open the seals, but no one can be found. John says, *I wept much that no one was found worthy to open the scroll* (Rev. 5:4). But the elder said, *Weep not; lo, the Lion of the tribe of Judah . . . has conquered, so that he can open the scroll* (Rev. 5:5). And when John turned to see the Lion, to his amazement he saw a Lamb, a Lamb with blood staining its neck, a Lamb that had been slain. As he watched, the Lamb stepped up to the throne and took the little book and all heaven broke into acclaim. Here at last was found One wise enough, strong enough and compassionate enough to solve the problems of man and to own the title deed of earth.

This is what the writer sees here in Hebrews. We see Jesus, who alone has broken through the barrier that keeps man from his heritage. What is that barrier? Have you ever analyzed that? What is it that keeps you from being what you want to be? What is it that keeps man from realizing his dreams of dominion? It is put in one grim word: death!

Death, in this passage as in many other places in Scripture, does not simply mean a funeral; it includes more than the ending of life. Death basically means uselessness; it means waste, futility. Death, in that sense, pervades all of life. You can see the signs of it all along. What is death? Boredom is death, and barrenness is death, as well as frustration and depression of spirit, anxiety, worry, fear, despair and defeat, along with all disease, all these are incipient death. The funeral is but the final straw. The closing of the casket is the ringing down of the curtain on a life of futility, of emptiness. The show is over! As Shakespeare put it,

"Life's but . . . a tale
Told by an idiot,
Full of sound and fury,
Signifying nothing."
(*Macbeth* 5. 5. 17)

The argument of Hebrews is that life apart from Jesus Christ is simply that kind of a tale. At the end of our life God may say, "It is a most remarkable performance, but the trouble is you missed the point. It signifies nothing."

But Jesus fulfilled the qualifications to realize man's heritage. He became lower than the angels, He took on flesh and blood, He entered into the human race to become part of it, He experienced death. Not only the death of the cross, but also that incipient death that marks the way of man through all his days. Thus He tasted death for every man, and in doing so He took our place. He thus made it possible for those who throw in their lot with Him to find that He has removed the thing that gives death its sting.

We shall see more of this in a moment, but for now it is enough to see that in Jesus Christ man has one ray of hope that he can realize the destiny God had provided for him. Christ has come to begin a new race of men. That race includes Himself and all those who are His, and to that race the promise is that they shall enter into all the fulness God ever intended man to have. Listen to the way Paul puts it to the Colossians, in Phillips' glowing translation. *They are those to whom God has planned to give a vision of the full wonder and splendor of his secret plan for the nations (sons of men). And the secret is simply this: Christ in you! Yes, Christ in you bringing with him the hope of all the glorious things to come.*[2] (Col. 1:27).

That is the first reason Christ became man: to recapture man's lost inheritance. Which Gospel does that agree to? The Gospel of Matthew, the Gospel of the great King.

The second reason why Christ became man is **to recover our lost unity.**

For it was fitting that he, for whom and by whom all things exist, in bringing many sons to glory, should make the pioneer of their salvation perfect through suffering. For he who sanctifies and those who are sanctified have all one origin. That is why he is not ashamed to call them brethren, saying, "I will proclaim thy name to my brethren, in the midst of the congregation I will praise thee." And again, "I will put my trust in him." And again, "Here am I, and the children God has given me."
(Heb. 2:10-13).

The earthly life of Jesus is referred to in one phrase, *made perfect through suffering.* Was He not perfect when He came? When Jesus was a babe in Bethlehem's manger, was He not perfect even then? When He was tempted in the desert and Satan tried to turn Him from the cross, was He not already perfect? When He was feeding the five thousand, in compassionate ministry to the hungry multitudes, was He not perfect? Why then does it say He must be perfected by suffering?

There are, of course, two perfections involved. He

was perfect in His person all along. The Scriptures make this abundantly clear. But He was not yet perfect in His work. Some of you young people may be perfect in health, perfect in body, perfect in strength, perfect in the soundness of your humanity, but you are not yet perfect in the work you are called to do. Suppose Jesus Christ had come full-grown into the world a week before He died. Suppose He had never been born as a baby, had never grown up into adult life, but had stepped into the earth full-grown as a man. Suppose He had uttered in one week's time the Sermon on the Mount, the Olivet discourse, the Upper Room discourse and all the teachings that we have from His lips recorded in Scripture. Imagine that He came on Monday and on Friday they took Him out and crucified Him, hanging Him on the cross, and that He died, just as it is recorded in the Scriptures, bearing the sins of the world. Would He still have been a perfect Saviour?

Certainly He would have been perfect as far as bearing our guilt is concerned: that only required a sinless Saviour. But He would not have been perfect as far as bearing our infirmities, our weaknesses, is concerned. He would have been able to fit us for heaven some day, but never able to make us ready for earth right now. In such a case we could always say (as too often we do say, anyway), "How can God expect me to live a perfect life in my situation? After all, I'm only human. Christ has never been where I am. What does He know of my pressures, what does He know of what I'm up against?" But He was made perfect through His suffering. He does know, He does know!

Some years ago a book was published with a characterization of Jesus on the cover. These words were written concerning Him: "A man who was often afraid, at a loss to know what was expected of him; a man who searched desperately for his own fulfillment and who, through his own strength and faith in divine guidance, conquered all human failings to set mankind an example it has never forgotten."

What is your reaction to that? Did you feel, as I felt when I first read it, that "This is but another example of liberal impertinence concerning Christ"? But when I read it through again I began to think about it, and soon found that I had only to change two words and I could accept it fully. I would have to take out the word "desperately"—"a man who searched desperately for his own fulfillment"—for I do not believe the Lord Jesus was ever desperate. And I would have to change the word "strength" to "weakness"—"Who, through his own 'weakness' and faith in divine guidance, conquered all human failings." But with those changes that is a perfectly accurate description of Jesus in His earthly life.

He was often afraid, He was uncertain at times, He searched for fulfillment in His life. If we deny Him this we deny Him His identification with us as human beings. These were the temptations He faced, the pressures He withstood. Every fear is temptation, every sense of uncertainty is temptation, and He was tempted "like as we are." Of course He never acted out of uncertainty, He never spoke out of fear, because He knew a secret, the secret He came to teach us: man is intended to be indwelt by God and to be continually dependent upon that God within him to give him everything he needs for every situation.

The moment Jesus felt fear gripping His heart, immediately He leaned back upon the full-flowing life of the indwelling Father and that fear was met by faith. The moment He felt uncertain, did not know which way to turn, He rested back upon the indwelling wisdom of God and was immediately given a word that was the right word for the situation. Because He fully entered into our fears and pressures He is fully one with us. That is why it can be recorded here, *For he who sanctifies and those who are sanctified have all one origin* (or are all one body, all one lump together).

The writer quotes from the Old Testament to illustrate the point, showing that the attitude and the relationship He had to God is the same we have to Him. *I will proclaim thy name to my brethren, in the midst of the congregation I will praise thee.* (Rejoicing in all things, that is to be our attitude.) And again, *I will put my trust in him.* (Trust is the secret of life.) And again, *Here am I, and the children God has given me.* (All one, together.)

Christ has become so utterly one with us and we with Him that all causes of division are removed, all ground of enmity is taken away, all disagreement is answered. Thus this passage links up with the Gospel of John, the Gospel of the one body, where Jesus prays to the Father, *that they may be one, even as we are one* (John 17:11). To make a new, wholly undivided body is the second reason Jesus Christ became man.

The third reason is to release us from our present bondage.

Since therefore the children share in flesh and blood, he himself likewise partook of the same nature, that through death he might destroy him who has the power of death, that is, the devil, and deliver all those who through fear of death were subject to lifelong bondage. (Heb. 2:14,15).

Is the devil destroyed? Do you think he has quit working? If we mean by this, "eliminated," obviously the answer is no. Bishop Pike said about the devil, "If there be such, he is still doing very well, as anyone reading the daily papers can know." Thus Pike disposed of the victory of Jesus Christ. But the word "destroy" here does not mean "eliminate." The word means "to render impotent; to nullify; to render inoperative, inconsequential." That is the idea. The devil has not been eliminated, but the devil has been rendered impotent. Not to everyone! Not to everyone! Only under certain conditions is this true, but those conditions are available to all men in Jesus Christ. That is what he is saying. When we enter into the conditions we discover that what he says is thrillingly true: there is a freeing from lifelong bondage.

The devil does not have the power of death in the sense of determining who dies and when life shall end. Only God has that power. But the phrase, "the power of death" means the grip of death, its fearsomeness, its terrible quality. Bondage therefore is that of the reign of sin, the flesh. This is what Paul means in Romans 8 when he says, *To set the mind on the flesh is death* (v. 6). Death is the absence of life. Death is not something in itself, it is simply the absence of something.

Someone gets hit by a car, the crowd gathers around and wonders if there is any life left. A doctor may come and examine the body. What does he look for? Evidences of death? No, he looks for evidences of life. If he can find no evidence of life as he searches the body of that person, he finally looks up and says, "I'm sorry; he's dead." Death, in all its forms, is absence of life. That is what boredom is, that is what distress is, that is what fear is, that is what anxiety is. These are forms of death because they are the absence of the life of the Lord Jesus.

It is from this death that Christ sets us free. The fear of this death is the devil's whip, the writer says, by which he keeps us in slavery and bondage all our life. Non-Christians, of course, have no escape from this, but even Christians, because they do not understand the kind of freedom that Christ brings, frequently experience death: defeat, waste, limitation, despair.

Let me give two examples. The first is taken from recent life, the realm of fact. It is the recent student unrest of the late Sixties on the campus of Berkeley and other universities. What was behind this? Why are students often so restless? The issue, as it was publicized in the papers, is the matter of freedom of speech and, in a sense, this is natural. Students are desirous of experiencing life, they want to live life to the full. Who does not? They want to experience life in the totality intended for man, and they equate such living with freedom. To a degree, this, too, is right, but the concepts of freedom may be wrong. I am not attempting to judge the situation. There was obviously right and wrong on both sides. But, in analyzing this, I see beneath the restlessness a constant hunger for life.

But to so hunger after life exposes us also to the devil's lie, that freedom is self-expression. It is having what *I* want; it is doing what *I* like; it is going where *I* want to go and acting as *I* please. It is the fear that we are going to miss out on life (the fear of death) that is the devil's whip to drive us into activity on a principle that leads us into more and greater death. To gain such freedom only means greater boredom; to be denied it means hate or despair, all forms of death.

Example number two: This comes from the realm of imagination, although it is often true. Here is a man who believes that money brings happiness, that if he can just get certain things in his life he will be content. Since he wants to be happy he devotes all his time to the unending contest to amass a fortune. As a result, life begins to pass him by more and more. He does not have time for the real things of life. In his grubby search for money and the things that money can buy he may awaken to find that the years have flown by and he has not yet begun to live. Because he is afraid that he will lose out on life he keeps this up, and in the end he loses out entirely. That is the devil's whip. These words are highly accurate, precisely stating the situation as it is being lived out day after day.

How does Christ deliver from this? The glory of the gospel of Jesus Christ is that the cross reverses our values. In its light we are able to strip away the devil's lie, and to act upon a totally different principle of life. That principle is this: freedom is not having what I want; it is doing what God wants. It is the man who gives up who gains; it is the man who flings away his life in abandonment to what God wants, who finally learns to live. It is the one who tries to keep his life who loses it. Is that not what Jesus said?

The man or woman who steps out upon this principle will discover that for him the devil is impotent. That man is set free to live the kind of life God intended him to live. He may not have some of the things others may have, for things do not produce happiness; but he has what God wants him to have: life lived to the fullest degree possible. That is the third reason Jesus Christ became man: to release us from the present bondage.

The last reason is to restore us in times of failure.

For surely it is not with angels that he is concerned but with the descendants of Abraham. Therefore he had to be made like his brethren in every respect, so that he might become a merciful and faithful high priest in the service of God, to make expiation for the sins of the people. For because he himself has suffered and been tempted, he is able to help those who are tempted (Heb. 2:16-18).

There is the cross again, *expiation for the sins of the people.* It comes at the end of a life in which the Lord Jesus learned to become a merciful and faithful high priest. The cross here is seen in its character as the basis for daily cleansing and forgiveness for the people of God. This has in view the ministry of 1 John 1:9. *If we confess our sins, he is faithful and just, and will forgive our sins and cleanse us from all unrighteousness.* He is able to do this because during His life He learned how to be merciful, that is, compassionate, and how to be faithful. That gracious compassion is now made available to us in His death. Christ's present attitude is summed up for us in Hebrews 5:2: *He can deal gently with the ignorant and wayward, since he himself is beset with weakness.*

If we come defending our sins, defiant, excusing ourselves, we can find no help at all. But if we come, as David comes in the Fifty-first Psalm, confessing, pouring it all out, admitting everything, saying it is wrong, and casting it all upon Him, we find there is an immediate flowing out of strength and healing, restoring grace.

Paul Fromer once wrote an editorial in *His* magazine in which he told of a personal incident in his own experience. He found himself bitter and resentful over a situation that had occurred in his work. As he thought over the hurtful attitudes others had shown toward him a verse from the Ninety-first Psalm flashed across his mind. *He who dwells in the shelter of the Most High, who abides in the shadow of the Almighty, will say to the Lord, "My refuge and my fortress; my God, in whom I trust"* (vv. 1,2).

He said it suddenly occurred to him that the verse was saying that Christ was not merely able to become a refuge and a fortress; He *is* that. As he went on, he said he thought of the Lord as across the room from him, a refuge, a fortress. But here Fromer was on this side and the problem was how to close the gap, how to get into the fortress, the place of refuge. As he thought further about his problem and what

Christ could be to him, the thought came to him, "Why not itemize your problem? You are dwelling on it in such a hazy, vague fashion. You must get it down to specifics. Now itemize it." So he did that and found that he had six grievances rather than one, as he thought when he started. Then he went through these six and, one by one, as he thought on each one, he felt the Lord imparting to him a different point of view. He began to look at each from the point of view of those who had caused his problem, and each time he saw there was some basis for their accusation. He was then able to forgive and forget each grievance.

Eventually, as he went down this list one by one he found every one of them was settled. When he reached the end he found that all the resentment had ebbed away and in its place was a sense of peace and quietness of heart that made him able to go back to his work without strain, fret, or distress. He realized then that Christ in His high priestly ministry had closed the gap and had made him discover that *He who dwells in the shelter of the Most High abides in the shadow of the Almighty.* If you learn the reality of this you will not need to go to a psychiatrist, or buy a book on peace of mind. If you know Jesus Christ you can come directly to Him, at any time, any place, and find that His ministry will bring you under the shadow of the Almighty.

The writer of this letter is deeply concerned that Christians enter into this relationship. And my question to you in this twentieth century hour is: How much have you discovered this total ministry of Christ in your own life? He became a man not only to recapture our lost destiny but also to heal the disagreements among us and bring us into the unity of one life in Him; to release us from daily, lifelong bondage to the fear of losing out on life; and to bring us that sweet, healing ministry which, in time of failure, restores us to fellowship without condemnation.

"Lord, teach us to be more than perfunctory about our prayers. Grant us depth, honesty, earnestness that we may believe this marvelous ministry made available to us by our Lord Jesus. That here in this twentieth century hour there may arise such a tremendous demonstration of what human life was intended to be that everywhere around men and women will be talking about it and saying, 'What do these people have?'

"We ask it in Christ's name,
Amen."

3

living out of rest

A group of tourists visiting the city of Rome came to an enclosure where a number of chickens were penned. The guide who was taking them through the city said, "These are very unusual and distinctive chickens. They happen to be descendants of the rooster that crowed on the night in which Peter denied the Lord." The tourists were very much impressed. One Englishman among them peered at the chickens and said, "My word! What a remarkable pedigree!" An American immediately reached for his checkbook and said, "How much do they cost?" But an Irishman turned to the guide and said, "Do they lay any eggs?" He was not interested in apostolic succession, but in apostolic success!

This is the attitude many have toward the Christian faith, and properly so. Can it do anything for me right now? Does the good news of the gospel have anything really helpful to say about the problem of nervous tension, for instance? Can it aid me in the matter of an inferiority complex? Will it do anything for my terrible habit of anxiety and worry when things do not go right? These are the problems that more desperately affect our lives than any other. We may be concerned about atomic bombs and nuclear warfare, but the problems of nervous tension and inferiority, resentment and bitterness, take their bitter toll of us each day.

Hebrews, chapter 2, closed on a practical note. The Lord Jesus, in His coming to earth, became a man for four mighty reasons. Among them, and the one last stated, was that He might be a compassionate and merciful High Priest in order that He might help those that are tempted, in the midst of their temptation. Chapter 3 picks up that theme and develops it, asking us to consider the astonishing solution that is offered by Jesus Christ to this plaguing, nagging problem of frustration, hypertension, anxiety, and all the neuroses and psychoses that are so familiar today.

Therefore, holy brethren, who share in a heavenly call, consider Jesus, the apostle and high priest of our confession. He was faithful to him who appointed him, just as Moses also was faithful in God's house. Yet Jesus has been counted worthy of as much more glory than Moses as the builder of a house has more honor than the house. (For every house is built by some one, but the builder of all things is God.) Now Moses was faithful in all God's house as a servant, to testify to the things that were to be spoken later, but Christ was faithful over God's house as a son. And we are his house if we hold fast our confidence and pride in our hope.
(Heb. 3:1-6).

Seven times in that short section the word "house" appears, and is primarily a reference to "God's house." There is a very common misunderstanding abroad today, especially among Christians, that the term "the house of God" means a church building. In my opinion there is nothing more destructive of the greatest message of the New Testament than that belief! A building is never truly called the house of God, either in the New Testament or the Old Testament, in the present or in the past. Certainly no church building, since the days of the early church, could ever properly be called the house of God. The early church never referred to any building in that way. As a matter of fact, the early church had no buildings for two or three hundred years. When they referred to the house of God they meant the people. A church is not a building, it is people!

Even the Temple or the Tabernacle of old was not really God's house. Let someone point out the fact that no building today can properly be called the house of God, and some Bible-instructed Christian nearby wisely nods his head and says, "Yes, you're right. The only building that could properly be called the house of God was the Temple or the Tabernacle." It is true that these buildings were termed that in Scripture, but it is meant only in figure, only as a picture. They were never actually meant to be the place where God dwelled.

In the sixty-sixth chapter of his magnificent prophecy, Isaiah records the words of the Lord, saying, *Heaven is my throne and the earth is my footstool; what is the house which you would build for me? . . . All these things my hand has made* (Isa. 66:1,2). Paul, in preaching to the Athenians, reminded them that *God . . . does not live in shrines made by man* (Acts 17:24). Even as he said those words the Temple was still standing in Jerusalem. No, God does not dwell in buildings.

Then what is the house of God that is mentioned here? The answer is very clearly stated in verse 6. *We are his house.* We people. God never intended to dwell in any building; He dwells in people, in men and women, in boys and girls. That is the divine intention in making men, that they may be the tabernacle of His indwelling. In that beautiful scene recorded in the twenty-first chapter of Revelation, the last chapter of the Bible, the mighty vision of the prophets is fulfilled, *Behold, the dwelling of God is with men* (Rev. 21:3). Paul refers to this in 1 Corinthians, *Do you not know that your body is a temple of the Holy Spirit within you, which you have from God?* (I Cor. 6:19). This is the focus toward which all Scripture is directed. God's purpose is to inhabit your body and to make you to be the manifestation of His life, the dwelling place of all that He is; so that, as Paul prays in Ephesians 3, *you may be a body wholly filled and flooded with God himself.* (See v. 19.) The great message of the gospel is that it takes God to be a man. You cannot be a man without God. It takes Christ to be a Christian, and when you put Christ into the Christian you put God back into the man. That is the good news, that is the gospel.

Now in this house of God, which is people, Moses ministered as a servant, but Christ as a Son. Therefore the Son is much more to be obeyed, much more to be listened to, much more to be honored and heeded, than the servant. Moses served faithfully as a servant. What is the ministry of a servant? A servant is always preparing things. He must prepare meals, he must prepare rooms, he must prepare the yard. He is always working in the anticipation of something yet to come. His work is in view of that which is yet future. So, *Moses was faithful in all God's house as a servant, to testify to the things that were to be spoken later* (*yet to come*), *but Christ was . . . as a Son* (Heb. 3:5,6).

What is the role of a son in a house? To take over everything, to possess it, to use whatever he likes. The house was made for him. So Christ has come to inhabit us, as Paul again prays in Ephesians, *that Christ may make his home in your hearts by faith.* (See Eph. 3:17.)

Now, the writer declares, *we are that house–if.* At this point he interjects the little word, *if. And we are his house if we hold fast our confidence and pride in our hope* (Heb. 3:6). And again in verse 14. *For we share in Christ, if only we hold our first confidence firm to the end.*

Now a cloud passes over the sun. The possibility is raised of being self-deceived in this matter of belonging to Christ, of being His house. It all hangs upon that word of uncertainty, *if.* What does this mean? Well, there are two possible views of this that are usually taken by Christians. There is the view that we can be built into the house of God and become part of it, that Christ can come to dwell in our hearts and we can be the tabernacle of the Most High, and then, later on, because we fail to lay hold of all that God gives us and we sin, we lose all we have gained, Christ leaves us and we lose our salvation. This is the view that is called "Arminianism" (not Armenianism) after a man named Arminius, a theologian in the Middle Ages. This view suggests that it is possible to lose our faith after we have once become the habitation of the Most High.

But if we take that view we are immediately in direct contradiction with some very clear and precise statements elsewhere that declare exactly the opposite. For instance, in John 10:27,28, Jesus said, *My sheep hear my voice, and I know them, and they follow me; and I give them eternal life, and they shall never perish.* Why? *My Father, who has given them to me, is greater than all, and no one is able to snatch them out of the Father's hand* (v. 29). Romans 8, verse 35, asks, *Who shall separate us from the love of Christ?* Paul goes on to list all the possibilities, then he declares, *No, in all these things we are more than conquerors through him who loved us* (v. 37).

Another possible meaning here suggests that, once having professed to receive the Lord Jesus, once having invited Him to come in, if then we do not manifest signs of new life, if nothing happens to our behavior as a result of our profession of faith, we have simply been self-deceived. We never had faith despite the external appearances, the religious observances that we have gone through. This is the danger the whole book of Hebrews faces. We will return to it again and again. Hebrews is addressed to a body of people among whom were certainly some whose Christian life was highly in doubt because they were not growing, they were not going on, they were not entering in to what God had provided for them.

This was not mere hypocrisy. The writer is not speaking of one who deliberately tries to pass himself off as a Christian, knowing in himself he is not. There are those who join a church because they think it is good for business or helps their status or prestige in the community, but they know they are not Christians. They do not believe what they hear, they do not have any interest in what is said. Such people stick out like sore thumbs among the saints. They deceive no one but themselves.

But the writer of Hebrews is talking here about some who have fallen into self-confident delusion and who feel themselves to be Christians. They have gone through every possible prescribed ritual to identify themselves with Christianity. Because of this they feel they are Christians. They believe the right things, they hold the right creed, they have orthodoxy in every bone of their body. They are rigid about the proclamation of the truth and conform to doctrine in every degree. But they are self-deceived. As they are unable to manifest what God has come into human hearts to produce, they reveal that there never was faith in the beginning. So, in Hebrews, continuance is the ultimate proof of reality.

An illustration confirms clearly the point. If it is properly understood, it is designed to shake us to our eyeteeth. It is the story of the rebellion of Israel in the wilderness.

Therefore, as the Holy Spirit says, "Today, when you hear his voice, do not harden your hearts as in the rebellion, on the day of testing in the wilderness, where your fathers put me to the test and saw my works

for forty years." Therefore I was provoked with that generation, and said, "They always go astray in their hearts; they have not known my ways." As I swore in my wrath, "They shall never enter my rest"
(Heb. 3:7-11).

Further, in verse 16,

Who were they that heard and yet were rebellious? Was it not all those who left Egypt under the leadership of Moses? And with whom was he provoked forty years? Was it not with those who sinned, whose bodies fell in the wilderness? And to whom did he swear that they should never enter his rest, but to those who were disobedient? So we see that they were unable to enter because of unbelief.
(Heb. 3:16-19).

The writer points out this people comprised almost the whole number of those who left Egypt under Moses. They had fulfilled every prescribed symbol of deliverance, but they were not delivered. While they were in Egypt they had killed the Passover lamb, and had sprinkled the blood of it over the doorposts. On the terrible night when the angel of death passed through the land and took the life of every first-born son in every household, they were safe. They had followed Moses as they left Egypt and had come to the borders of the Red Sea. As the waters flowed before them and the armies of the Egyptians were fast approaching from the rear, Moses lifted up his rod and the waters parted and they all passed through the sea as well. As Paul says in 1 Corinthians, *they were baptized into Moses in . . . the sea* (1 Cor. 10:2). They were united to him.

Many of us, perhaps, have likewise looked to the cross of Christ and in some degree counted His death as valid for us as the blood of our Passover lamb. We have gone through the waters of baptism, testifying by that that we believe we have been baptized by the Spirit of God into the body of Christ, made to be part of Him.

These people, as they wandered through the wilderness on the way from Egypt to Canaan, had enjoyed the protection and guidance of the pillar of fire by night and the cloud by day, speaking of the protection, guidance, and fatherly care of God. They had even been fed every day by the manna as it came from the skies, fresh every morning. Centuries later, when the Jews of our Lord Jesus' day heard Him refer to them as children of the devil, they said to Him, "We are not children of the devil, we are children of Abraham. Don't you know what happened to our fathers? Talk about people of God! We are the true people of God. Our fathers ate bread in the wilderness for forty years: if that is not a sign that we are the people of God, I don't know what could be!" But the writer says, *With whom was he provoked forty years? Was it not with those who sinned, whose bodies fell in the wilderness?* (Heb. 3:17).

When the test finally came and they stood on the borders of the Promised Land, they were given the word of the Lord through Moses to advance and take the land. But they held back because they were afraid of the giants that inhabited the cities of that land. When they were asked to face the giants and, by the principle of faith, to overcome them and enter into the rest of the land, they refused to do so. They turned back and for forty years wandered in the wilderness. The test came when for the first time they were asked to come to grips with the thing that could destroy their life in the land, the giants, and their failure to do so revealed the bitter truth that they never had any faith. They had never really believed God. They were only acting as they did to escape the damage, death, and danger of Egypt. But they had no intention of coming into conflict with the giants in the land.

The Word of God is pointing out to us that we may profess the Lord Jesus, we may take our stand in some outward way at least upon the cross of Christ and claim His death for us. We can profess to have been baptized into His body, and say so by passing through the waters of baptism ourselves. We can enjoy the fatherly care and providence of God and see Him working miracles of supply in our life, and even find in the Scripture much which sustains the heart, at least for awhile. Yet, when it comes to the test, when God asks us to lay hold of the giants in our life which are destroying us; those giants of anxiety, fear, bitterness, jealousy, envy, impatience, and all the other things that keep us in turmoil and make us to be a constant trouble to our neighbors and friends–when we are asked to lay hold of these by the principle of faith and we refuse to do so, the writer says we are in danger of remaining in the wilderness and never entering the promised rest.

Take care, brethren, lest there be in any of you an

evil, unbelieving heart, leading you to fall away from the living God. But exhort one another every day, as long as it is called "today," that none of you may be hardened by the deceitfulness of sin. For we share in Christ, if only we hold our first confidence firm to the end.
(Heb. 3:12-14).

We share in Christ if that faith which began in us continues to produce in us that which faith alone can produce, the fruit of the Spirit. This is the second warning of this book. The first one was against drifting, the danger of paying no attention, of sitting in a meeting and letting the words flow by while our minds are occupied elsewhere. That is the peril of letting these magnificent truths, which alone have power to set men free, drift by unheeded, unheard.

This second warning is against the danger of hardening: of hearing the words and believing them, understanding what they mean, but taking no action upon them. The peril of holding truth in the head but never letting it get into the heart. Truth known never does anything; it is truth done which sets us free. Truth known simply puffs us up in pride of knowledge. We can quote the Scriptures by the yard, can memorize it, can know the message of every book and know the whole Book from cover to cover, but truth known will never do anything for us. It is truth done, truth acted upon, that moves and delivers and changes.

The terrible danger which the writer is pointing out is: that truth that is known but not acted on has an awful effect of hardening the heart so that it is no longer able to act, and we lose the ability to believe. This is what the Lord Jesus meant when He said to His disciples, *If they do not hear Moses and the prophets, neither will they be convinced if some one should rise from the dead* (Luke 16:31).

A man once said to me, "If we only had the ability to do miracles like the early church did, then we could really make this Christian cause go. If we could perform these things again, and had faith enough to do miracles, we could make people believe." But I had to tell him that after thirty years of observing this scene and studying the Scriptures I am absolutely convinced that if God granted us this power, as He is perfectly able to do, so that miracles were being demonstrated on every hand, there would not be one further Christian added to the cause of Christ than there is right now!

At the close of Jesus' own ministry, after that remarkable demonstration of the power of God in the midst of people, how many stood with Him at the foot of the cross? A tiny band of women and one man, and they had been won, not by His miracles, but by His words. This is why God says, *I swore in my wrath, "They shall never enter my rest."* That is not petulance. That does not mean God is upset because He has offered something and they will not take it. That is simply a revelation of the nature of the case. When truth is known and not acted upon, it always–on every level of life, in any area of human knowledge–has this peculiar quality: it hardens, so the heart is finally not able to believe what it refuses to act on.

Now we come to the sign of reality. What is it

that unmistakably marks the one who has genuinely become part of God's house? What is the "rest" of God, the mark of reality?

Therefore, while the promise of entering his rest remains, let us fear lest any of you be judged to have failed to reach it. For good news came to us just as to them; but the message which they heard did not benefit them, because it did not meet with faith in the hearers.
(Heb. 4:1,2).

That does not mean the message did not meet with belief. When the Israelites stood at the borders of the land they had no doubts at all that the land was there, they believed in it. Nor was it that they did not believe there was honey and milk in the land, the fulness of supply awaiting them; they believed it. There was a species of belief, but there was no faith, for faith is more than belief. Faith is action upon that belief! There was belief, there was even strong desire to enter the land, but they did not enter because they had no faith. They would not act upon that which had been given.

The writer says the same gospel was given to us as to them; we have the same good news, the same possibility of entering into a life of rest. These words must be taken seriously. The Word of God knows nothing of the easy believism that is so widely manifest in our own day. We think we can receive Jesus as Saviour, raise our hand to accept Christ, and that settles the matter. We will go to heaven and there can never be any doubt about it from then on, though there is no change in our life. But the promise of Christ is that when He comes into the human heart there is a radical change of government which must inevitably, in the course of its working, result in a revolutionary change in behavior. Unless that takes place there has been no reality to our conversion. The goal of His working in us is rest.

Now what is this rest? In verse 3 we learn it is pictured for us by the Sabbath.

For we who have believed enter that rest, as he has said, "As I swore in my wrath, They shall never enter my rest," although his works were finished from the foundation of the world. [Here is a rest that has been available to man ever since man first appeared on earth. It was available from the foundation of the world.] *For he has somewhere spoken of the seventh day in this way, "And God rested on the seventh day from all his works." And again in this place he said, "They shall never enter my rest."*
(Heb. 4:3-5).

You know the story of creation. On the seventh day God ceased from His labors; He rested on the seventh day, intending that to be a picture of what the rest of faith is. It has been available to man since the beginning of the world. Certain groups have focused upon the shadow instead of the substance and have insisted that we must observe the Sabbath day much as it was given to Israel; that this is what pleases God. But God is never pleased by the perfunctory observance of shadows, of figures.

Here is one of the great problems of Christian faith.

We are constantly mistaking shadows for substance, pictures for reality. A teen-age girl told me, in an anguish of repentance, that she had gotten up from a Communion service and gone out to engage in some very wrong activities. When I said to her, "How could you do this? How could you leave a Communion service to do this?" she replied, defensively, "Well, I didn't partake of Communion." And I said, "What difference does that make?" That was a mere shadow. Communion pictures the sharing of the life of the Lord Jesus, and if we deny that in our activity but are scrupulous about its observance in the shadow, in the mere picture, it is an insult to God.

The believer's rest was figured in the Sabbath; and anyone who learns to live out of rest is keeping the Sabbath as God meant it to be kept. It was also prefigured in the land of Canaan, yet in verse 8 it says, *If Joshua had given them rest, God would not speak later of another day.* If the figure had been enough God would not, later on in the Scriptures, have recorded the words, *there remains a sabbath rest for the people of God* (v. 9). Obviously, Canaan, too, was nothing but a figure, nothing but a picture, a shadow. Then what is the real rest? We come to it in verse 10; it is most clearly stated. *For whoever enters God's rest also ceases from his labors as God did from his.*

Here is a revolutionary new principle of human behavior on which God intends man to operate. That was His intention from the beginning. It is from this that man fell and it is to this now, in Jesus Christ, he is to be restored. Unless this principle is operative in our life we can have no assurance that we belong to the body of Christ. This is the clear declaration of this writer throughout the whole of the book.

We all have been brainwashed since birth with a false concept of the basis of human activity. We have been sold on the satanic lie that we have in ourselves what it takes to be what we want to be, to be a man, to be a woman, to achieve whatever we desire. We are sure we have what it takes or, if we do not have it now, we know where we can get it. We can educate ourselves, we can acquire more information, we can develop new skills, and when we get this done we shall have what it takes to be what we want to be.

For three and a half years the apostle Peter tried his level best to please the Lord Jesus by dedicated, earnest, sincere efforts to serve Him out of his own will. He failed dismally, because he could not be convinced that he did not have what it takes. When the Lord Jesus told him, "You will never have what it takes until the cross comes into your life," he would not receive it. He said, "Lord, don't talk to me about a cross. I don't want to hear anything about that."

And the Lord Jesus said, "Get behind Me, Satan, you are an offense unto Me. You do not understand the things of God, but only the things of men." It was not until that wonderful day, the day of Pentecost, when the Holy Spirit opened his eyes to the full meaning of the cross, that he realized what the Lord had meant. Not till then did he realize what it took to be a Christian.

We repeat, it takes Christ to be a Christian, and it takes God to be a man. When you put Christ back in the Christian, you put God back in the man. This is God's design for living. This is the new principle of human activity–to stop our own efforts. We do not have what it takes, and we never did have. The only One who can live the Christian life is Jesus Christ. He proposes to reproduce His life in us. Our part is to expose every situation to His life in us and by that means, depending upon Him and not upon us, we are to meet every situation, enter into every circumstance, and perform every activity. We cease from our own labors.

This is the way you began the Christian life, if you are a Christian. You came to the place where you stopped trying to save yourself, did you not? You quit trying to be good enough to get to heaven. You said, "I'll never make it, I'll never make it." You looked to the Lord Jesus and said, "If He has taken my place, then that is all I need." Thus, receiving Him and resting on that fact by faith, you stopped your own efforts, you ceased from your own work and rested on His. Now Paul says in Colossians, *As therefore you received Christ Jesus the Lord, so live in him* (Col. 2:6). "As . . . so," in the same way. As you have received Him, so live in dependence upon Him to do all things through you. Step out upon that, and what is the result? Rest! Wonderful rest! Relief, release, no longer worrying, fretting, straining, for you are resting upon One who is wholly adequate to do through you everything that needs to be done. He does not make automatons of us, He does not turn us into robots. He works through our thinking, our feeling and our reasoning, but our dependence must be upon Him.

Notice the word that is stressed through this whole section: today. This is God's design for living today.

It is not inactivity, but it is freedom from strain. It is the principle upon which He expects everything to be done: your work, your schooling, your studies, your play, your responsibilities in the home, at the shop, wherever you are. All are to be fulfilled out of reliance upon this new principle of human behaviour. *Whatever you do, in word or deed, do everything in the name of* (by the authority and ability of) *the Lord Jesus* (Col. 3:17).

Now one final word on how. If you have never yet entered into this principle in any degree and yet have been truly born of God by the Holy Spirit, this study will find you asking, "Lord, show me how. I want to enter into this rest, I want to know what this is." Then look at the instrument by which we enter in, the Word of God.

Let us therefore strive to enter that rest, that no one fall by the same sort of disobedience. For the Word of God is living and active, sharper than any two-edged sword, piercing to the division of soul and spirit, of joints and marrow, and discerning the thoughts and intentions of the heart.
(Heb. 4:11,12).

In order to enter into this new principle we must repudiate the old. But the problem is, the old basis of activity is so ingrained in our thinking that we automatically respond to old thought-patterns. Thus, though the new life of the Lord Jesus may be in us, we find ourselves repudiating it and responding along old lines, reacting in bitterness, impatience, anger, frustration, anxiety, worry, fear, trepidation, uncertainty and inferiority. We do not know how to recognize the old in its practical appearance. What will help us? The Word of God! This living, marvelous Word becomes an instrument in the hands of the Holy Spirit with a two-edged action. It strips off the false. If we seek to obey it as we read it, we shall discover that it exposes the entrenched power of the flesh in our life and strips off all pretense. It is not only the Bible which is meant by the phrase *the word of God.* It is the truth of God, whether it comes by sermon, by Scripture, or by some confirmation of life. It is the truth that strips off the false. It can be utterly ruthless, moving it on us, backing us into a corner, taking down all our fences and facades, worming its way right into the heart of our nature, discerning even between the soul and the spirit. One time I watched the book of Esther in the hands of the Holy Spirit take a group of people and strip off their pretenses and expose them to themselves. For the first time they saw, with horror, what they really were under the domination of this sin-principle, the flesh.

But the Word has a twofold action. It not only strips off the false, but it unveils the true. When we come to the place where, like Jacob, we are ready to take a good look at ourselves, then there comes the marvelous, healing, wholesome, comforting, sweet, delivering Word that sets us on our feet again, and shows us, in Christ, every provision for every need. We need no longer to go on doggedly, wearily fighting a battle that is already lost, but we can step out each fresh, new day into the glorious experience of a victory that is already won.

And what is the final outcome? Look at verse 13.

And before him no creature is hidden, but all are open and laid bare to the eyes of him with whom we have to do.

We come at last to the God of reality. When Adam sinned, he hid from God. He hid because he realized he was naked; he was ashamed, and he clothed himself. When all pretense is stripped off and we see ourselves for what we are, and by faith have appropriated what Christ is; when we believe that He not only died for us, but rose again to live in us; when we realize that we not only need Him for what He did, but also for what He is; then we can stand again before God exactly as we are, naked, without need of facades, masks, or pretenses. We are exactly what we are, that is all, just men, just women, just sinners saved by grace, with nothing to defend, nothing that need be hidden, nothing that cannot be fully exposed to everyone. We discover a wonderful lifting of burdens, a wonderful freedom, a wonderful release—we have entered into rest. The fences come down between us and our friends and neighbors; we do not try to hide anything any more. Because we are what we are before God, we can be exactly what we are before men.

Perhaps you have been in the wilderness a long, long time—too long. Normally, as this book will make clear as we go on, it is expected that a Christian who comes to know the Lord Jesus will be led into the experience of rest within a few years after his conversion. It may take no longer than a few months. But even if you have been living in the wilderness of self-effort for many years, it is yet possible to die to your unbelief, as that old generation died, to leave the carcass of unbelieving self-sufficiency behind, and, like the new generation born in the wilderness to follow your heavenly Joshua into the land.

You cannot crucify the flesh; that God has already done. But you can agree to it. And when you do, you will discover this priceless gift of peace, of rest. But if you refuse, knowing what to do but not willing to do it, the living death that marks your fruitless, crabbed, self-centered, so-called "Christian" life, will be the tombstone of a phony faith, a faith that never really was, a house built upon the sand, which, when the floods and storms of life strike it, is swept to destruction.

"Lord Jesus, how this Word has searched our hearts. We have found it to be exactly what You have declared it to be, that which can pierce even the joints and the marrow, discerning the thoughts and intents of the heart. Thank You for this wonderful surgery that sets us free. We rejoice that there is a rest remaining into which we can enter. Grant us that we shall.
In Your name,
Amen."

4

strength at wit's end

In our last chapter we learned of a new and radical principle of human behavior which every true Christian will learn and practice in this present life, or the absence of it will prove he has never had a real conversion and has no right to call himself a Christian. This principle, then, is not an option. It is not something we can choose to accept or ignore. It is the whole goal of God's work in human hearts. This principle is called in Hebrews *the rest of God;* it is activity out of rest. It is to cease from our self-directed activities, the principle upon which we have lived our human lives ever since we were babies, convinced that we had what it takes to do what we wanted to do or, at least, could get what it takes from some human source. This new principle, made available to us only in Jesus Christ, means to cease our self-directed activities and to trust in the ability of a second Person to work through us.

That is exactly what faith is. Every one of you exercises faith every time you sit in a chair. You trust in the work of another person. You don't pick up a chair and examine it to see if it will support you if you sit on it. You take it by faith; you exercise trust in the maker of the chair. You may not have the least idea who he is, whether he is a rascal or trustworthy, but you simply take it for granted and exercise a faith which supports you. We make faith so difficult but it is simply trusting in the work of another.

And that is what the life of rest is: trusting the Lord Jesus who has come to indwell our hearts to do through us all that we do, using the functions of our human personality to do so. That is rest. It takes away from us our favorite excuse for failure. It demands we stop justifying our failure by saying, "Well after all, I'm only human." For this principle proposes to meet every situation, not with human wisdom, but with divine; not with human strength, but with God's strength; not by the exercise of sheer will power, but by the exercise of absolute trust.

The previous section in Hebrews closed with chapter 4, verse 13. *And before him no creature is hidden, but all are open and laid bare to the eyes of him with whom we have to do.*

This One *with whom we have to do,* Jesus Christ, knows us thoroughly, sees everything about us. Nothing is hidden from His gaze: we are absolutely open and naked before Him. He knows our weaknesses. He knows that when temptation is heavy upon us, when we are being harassed and irritated by the children or the boss or our mother-in-law, we shall be strongly tempted to give way, to fight back, to lose our temper and say things we ought not. The

Lord knows that when we are treated unfairly—perhaps we have done the right thing but are blamed for it, even insulted over it—there is a strong, almost overpowering urge to strike back, to get even, to do something to even the score. He knows that there is in the human heart a great hunger for acceptance by those around us, that we are very uncomfortable when we are in a crowd of people and feel we must act differently. He knows, too, that under those circumstances of pressure we will tend to excuse our failure by saying, "Well, I know I should lean on the Lord, but the provocation here is too great. I can take it up to a point, but if it gets too strong, I know I will give in."

Because of this tendency to excuse ourselves when the pressure gets too great, the writer now says in effect, "I want you to take a closer look at the great High Priest who is our strength, our refuge, our fortress, our enabler."

Since then we have a great high priest who has passed through the heavens, Jesus, the Son of God, let us hold fast our confession. For we have not a high priest who is unable to sympathize with our weaknesses, but one who in every respect has been tempted as we are, yet without sinning. Let us then with confidence draw near to the throne of grace, that we may receive mercy and find grace to help in time of need.
(Heb. 4:14-16).

Four words in that brief passage sum up all it has to say: "the throne of grace." It is fashionable in some circles these days to view the Protestant Reformation as a great mistake, something that we should feel ashamed of and work to heal by the ecumenical movement of our day.

It is interesting to note that wherever there has been genuine renewal in the Catholic Church (or the Protestant Church), it has been by a return to the great principles of the Reformation reflected in this passage. The reformers, Luther, Zwingli, Calvin and others, nailed to the masthead of their movement three great principles taken from the Scriptures. No sacrifice but Calvary; no priest but Christ; no confessional but the throne of Grace! With these three mighty principles they turned Europe upside down during the Middle Ages. The Christian finds power only as there is a return to these great things declared here.

Here is the throne of grace. A throne speaks of authority and power, while grace conveys the idea of sympathy and understanding. These two thoughts are combined in Jesus Christ. He is a man of infinite power, yet in complete and utter sympathy with us. He said Himself, after His resurrection, *All power is given unto me in heaven and in earth*[1] (Matt. 28:18). His title here in Hebrews is *Jesus, the Son of God,* possessing the fulness of deity.

But more than that, He is the One who has *passed through the heavens.* In this space age this phrase should catch our eye. Jesus not only passed into the heavens but through the heavens. This is the point the writer is making.

When we put men into a rocket and hurl them into space from Cape Canaveral, we throw them into the heavens. They are still within this space-time continuum. Even when they land on the moon this is true. It would still be true if they went to the nearest planets or the outermost reaches of our solar system.

But the claim made for Jesus is that He has passed through the heavens, He has passed outside the limits of time and space. He is no longer contained within or limited by those boundaries that hold us within physical limits. Because He is outside, above, beyond and over all, there are no limits to His power.

It is wrong to think of heaven in terms of space. There is a tendency for some Christians to think of heaven as "out there" in space somewhere, perhaps on one of the stars, some great distance from earth. Because of the figurative language employed in Scripture we think of going "up" to heaven and "down" to hell. It was this that Bishop Robinson seized upon in his book *Honest to God* and pushed to unwarrantable extremes.

The idea that is conveyed to us by the figurative language of the Scriptures is that heaven is outside time and space; therefore, it can be within us as well as around us, above us, and beyond us, since it is a dimension of reality beyond time and space limitations. The throne of grace is not a remote space; it is right in the heart of a believer in whom Jesus Christ dwells. To come to the throne of grace does not mean to go into a prayer closet and then address an appeal across the reaches of space to some distant point in heaven. It means to reckon upon the One who indwells us. The throne of grace is that close to us, that available to us.

The writer also makes clear that though the Lord Jesus has passed into the place of supreme power, and has absolutely no limits upon His ability to work, He also is tremendously concerned with our problems. He says, *We have not an high priest which cannot be touched with the feeling of our infirmities*[1] (Heb. 4:15). It is almost an indignant retort to some sly accusation, "We do not have," he says, "a priest who is remote from us, who is isolated from us, who does not understand what we are going through." Previously in this letter Jesus has been called "the pioneer of our salvation." This is the thought of the phrase here. He has already gone the whole course before us. He has felt every pressure, He has known every pull, He has been drawn by every allurement we face, He has been frightened by every fear, beset by every anxiety, depressed by every worry. Yet He did it without failure, without sinning. Never once did He fall. *Therefore,* the writer says, *let us draw near with boldness, with confidence to the throne of grace, that we may receive mercy and find grace to help every time we need it.* That is, all the time. Every help you need, every time you need it!

Now it is right at this point that the tempter pulls the neatest trick of the year. He suggests to us Christians that we file this verse away in our conscious mind as a creed to which we pay lip service. We say to each other, "Yes, it is true, Jesus has been tempted in every point as we have, yet without sin." We take that out and quote it any time we are exposed to doctrinal questioning. We especially love to quote it to others. But the tempter, at the same time, jams into our subconscious mind a very slimy doubt. He suggests to us a limitation which we hardly let ourselves think about: that there is one area in which

Jesus did not undergo the same temptation we have. "Of course Jesus never failed," the devil suggests, "because He had one great advantage over you: He had no sin nature."

It is true that Jesus was not beset by the devilish pull of sin in the flesh, such as we experience. His virgin birth protected Him from that. Therefore, deep in our subconscious, hardly allowing it to come to the surface, we feel there is pressure we can undergo that He has never felt, that there is power exerted upon us that He does not understand. That doubt pops out in times of pressure and says to us, "Go on, give in! You can't fight this to the end. You're weak in this area. You haven't the strength to stand. The Lord will forgive you, for, after all, that's His job, so go ahead and give in. You are too weak, too human to resist."

To answer that subtle argument fully, the writer brings before us the qualifications of a high priest. These are now briefly set before us.

For every high priest chosen from among men is appointed to act on behalf of men in relation to God, to offer gifts and sacrifices for sins. He can deal gently with the ignorant and wayward, since he himself is beset with weakness. Because of this he is bound to offer sacrifice for his own sins as well as for those of the people. And one does not take the honor upon himself, but he is called by God, just as Aaron was.
(Heb. 5:1-4).

We can dispose of this rather briefly. The writer is not speaking of Jesus Christ, he is listing the regulations, the qualifications, the requisites to be a priest in Israel. Here we learn what a priest really is. Perhaps you think of a priest as a man wearing a long, black robe, with his collar turned backwards, but that has nothing to do with priesthood. Perhaps you think the purpose of a priest is to baptize, marry, and bury or, as someone has put it, "to hatch, match, and dispatch." But that is not the task of a priest. The qualifications for a priest are right here.

A priest must first be a man, in order to represent men. To this end the Lord Jesus laid aside His glory as God, though He was equal with God, as Paul tells us, and humbled Himself and became a man. He entered the human race as a babe in Bethlehem. Second, a priest must offer sacrifices; that is, he must deal with the problem that separates man from God. He must come to grips with the awful universal problem of guilt, for this is the cloud over our lives that haunts us, stays with us, dogs our footsteps, and brings us into bondage every way we turn. It is universal among men. No man has ever been known that does not have and suffer from a sense of guilt. The answer to guilt is a life sacrificed, and a priest must therefore offer sacrifice. The Lord Jesus eminently and adequately fulfilled this requirement in His cross when He Himself became not only the priest, but the victim. He offered Himself, through the eternal Spirit of God, as a sacrifice for the guilt of men.

The third qualification of a priest is that he must himself be beset with weakness and sin in order that he might understand the problems of others. Here is the problem, is it not? How could Jesus Christ fulfill this and still be sinless? How could He live as a man and never sin, and yet understand how we feel when we sin? This is the area the enemy seizes upon to dislodge our faith when we come into times of intense pressure and trial. We will return to this in a moment, for this is the whole point of the passage.

The fourth qualification of a priest is that he must be appointed by God. *One does not take the honor upon himself, but he is called by God, just as Aaron was.* No man can ordain priests, only God can. The purpose of a priest, then, is to cleanse and strengthen, to make us fit for life. If a priest does not do that, he is worthless. He must make men fit for life.

The last section reveals the credentials of Jesus, the way He fully and adequately met every requirement of priesthood.

So also Christ did not exalt himself to be made a high priest, but was appointed by him who said to him, "Thou art my Son, today I have begotten thee"; as he says also in another place, "Thou are a priest for ever, after the order of Melchizedek"
(Heb. 5:5,6).

Those two quotations answer to points one and four of the qualifications we have listed. Begotten as a babe in the womb of Mary and born in Bethlehem, Jesus became a man, fully one with us in the essential humanity of our life. At the age of thirty He entered upon the priesthood; not the priesthood of Aaron but a new order called "Melchizedek" of which we will learn much more as we go on in Hebrews. This priesthood was predicted in the Scriptures and fulfilled when Jesus entered into His ministry and set about to do His Father's will. He was appointed by God unto this work.

The next verses take up the crucial matter. How could He never sin yet fully sympathize with sinners?

In the days of his flesh, Jesus offered up prayers and supplications, with loud cries and tears, to him who was able to save him from death, and he was heard for his godly fear. Although he was a Son, he learned obedience through what he suffered; and being made perfect he became the source of eternal salvation to all who obey him, being designated by God a high priest after the order of Melchizedek.
(Heb. 5:7-10).

How can He sympathize, how does He understand our pressures, if He has never sinned? The answer to that leads us into the dark shadows of Gethsemane. There is no other incident in the Gospels that fits the description of this passage where, with prayers and supplications, with loud cries and tears, He cried unto Him who was able to save Him from death. As the Lord and His disciples left the Upper room they passed through the dark valley of the Kidron, up onto the side of the Mount of Olives to the olive tree grove where it was His custom to go. Selecting three of the more sensitive of the disciples, Peter, James and John, He withdrew with them into the deeper shadows of the garden. There followed a protracted period of excruciating torment of spirit that found expression in loud, involuntary cries, streaming tears, and ending in a terrible bloody sweat.

Here we come face to face with mystery. There

is, first, the total unexpectedness of this to the Lord. He had gone to the garden as was His custom, but there He suddenly began to be greatly distressed and troubled. Nothing like this is recorded of Him before. In His anticipation of what He would be going through and His explanations of it to the disciples, He had never once mentioned Gethsemane. Furthermore, there is no prediction of this in the Old Testament. There is much that predicts what He would go through on the cross; there is not one word of what He endured in the garden.

In the midst of His bafflement, puzzlement, deep unrest of heart and distress of soul, He does an unusual and amazing thing. For the first time in His ministry he appealed to His own disciples for help. He said to them, *Watch with me, pray with me.* He asked them to bear Him up in prayer as He went further into the shadows, falling first to His knees and then to His face, crying out before the Father. There He prayed three separate times and each prayer is a questioning of the necessity of this experience. *My Father, if it be possible, let this cup pass from me* (Matt. 26:39). He was beseeching the Father to make clear to Him whether this was a necessary activity, so unexpected was this, so suddenly had it come upon Him, baffling Him, confusing Him, bewildering Him, just as sudden experiences and catastrophies come bewilderingly to us.

To deepen the mystery of this experience, there is the awful intensity of this struggle. This passage in Hebrews clearly implies that the Lord Jesus is here facing the full misery which sin produces in the heart of the sinner while he is yet alive, what we call "the sense of sin." I think we can even analyze this further. The threefold period of wrestling in the garden suggests that He was here being exposed to the full intensity of what makes sin in our lives so defeating, so unshakable, that which makes up a sense of sin: shame, guilt, and despair.

What is shame? Who of us has not felt it? Shame is a sense of my own defilement. It is an awareness of my unfitness. It is self-contempt, a loathing of myself. It is not being able to look myself in the face because I have been false to my standards, my ideals. As the Lord Jesus went into the darkness of the garden and fell upon His face, suddenly, for the first time in His experience, He began to feel ashamed. All the naked filth of human depravity forced itself upon Him and He felt the burning, searing shame of our misdeeds as though they were His. No wonder He trembled in agony and amazement and sought to flee. He cried to the Father, *My Father, if it be possible, let this cup pass from me.* He adds, *Nevertheless not my will, but thine, be done* (Luke 22:42).

Remember that He came then to the disciples and woke them with an almost piteous plea to watch with Him. *Could you not watch with me one hour?* He said (Matt. 26:40). Returning again to the shadows, a greater inward horror came upon Him. He began to feel a sense of guilt. What is guilt? Guilt is the sense of injury done to someone else. Guilt is the awareness of damage that I have caused to the innocent or the undeserving. The Lord Jesus was borne to the ground by an overwhelming sense of dark and awful guilt. He felt Himself a culprit before God. He felt Himself a child of wrath, eminently deserving judgment. He writhed in silent torment among the olives, and Matthew tells us He began to pray more earnestly than ever before, *O my Father, if this cup may not pass away from me, except I drink it, thy will be done*[1] (Matt. 26:42).

Once again He came to His disciples and, finding them sleeping, He went back. He did not awaken them but let them sleep on. The third experience of agony was the worst of all. Before it began the Father sent an angel to strengthen Him. This is what is meant by the words, *He was heard for his godly fear* (Heb. 5:7). He cried out to the Father in His deep and desperate need, and the Father answered and strengthened Him through an angel. When the angel had finished ministering to Him, the third and most terrible experience began. Our Lord began to know despair.

He fully felt the iron bands of sin's enslaving power. He was crushed under a sense of hopelessness, of helpless discouragement, of utter defeat. His eyes filled with tears. His mouth was opened in involuntary, agonized cries. His heart was crushed as in a winepress, so that the blood was literally forced from His veins and His sweat fell to the ground in great, bloody drops. This explains the strange words, *Although he was a Son, he learned obedience through what he suffered* (Heb. 5:8).

He learned what it means to obey God when every cell in His body wanted to disobey, when everything within Him cried out to flee this experience. Yet, knowing this to be the will of God, He obeyed, trusting God to see Him through. He learned what it feels like to hang on when failure makes us want to throw the whole thing over, when we are so defeated, so utterly despairing, so angry with ourselves, so filled with shame, self-loathing and guilt that we want to forget the whole thing. He knows what that is like; He went the whole way; He took the full brunt of it. You and I will never pass through a Gethsemane like He went through. He went the whole distance.

Verse 9 carries us on to the cross. *Being made perfect*–having entered into all that any sinner in all his weakness ever knows–*being made perfect he became the source of eternal salvation to all who obey him.* That is the language of discipleship. When we obey Him as He obeyed the Father, then all that God is, is made available to us, just as in the hour of His anguish all that God is, was made available to Him on this principle of trust.

How did He win? On the same principle that is set before us. He absolutely refused to question the Father's wisdom. He refused to strike back at God, to blame Him, to say this was unfair. He took no refuge in unbelief even though this trial came suddenly and unexpectedly upon Him. Instead, He cast Himself upon the Father's loving, tender care and looked to Him to sustain Him. When He did, He was brought safely through and was thus perfected for priesthood. So we read, *Let us then with confidence draw near to the throne of grace, that we may receive mercy and find grace to help in time of need* (Heb. 4:16). No matter how deep, how serious that need may be, He can fully meet it, though we may be at wit's end.

In Psalm 107 there is a wonderful statement: *They*

. . . were at their wits' end. Then they cried to the Lord in their trouble, and he delivered them from their distress (Ps. 107:27,28).

It is at wits' end, driven by the Spirit into the place where the pressure is so great that we have no other recourse but to cry out to God for help, that at last we begin to learn. It breaks upon our dull, slow minds that this help is not something intended for emergency situations only. This dependence on Him is the principle upon which God expects us to meet every circumstance. It is thus we enter into rest.

"Our Father, Thank You that the garden of Gethsemane was not mere play acting upon a stage. The Lord Jesus did not come into the world to perform a role; He fully entered into life. He went the whole way, He bore the full brunt. Help us, then to obey these simple words of admonition: to come with confidence, with boldness to the throne of grace that is within us from which all help comes, all light is streaming, all hope is flaming. Make these words real in our experience. In Christ's name, Amen."

5

let's get on with it

The passage before us is so important and so provocative that I will waste no time in introduction. I shall follow the suggestion of our title and "get on with it." The section from Hebrews 5:11 to 6:12 gathers around four figures or pictures, though one is implied rather than stated. We shall call these four figures the milk drinkers, the meat eaters, the stillborn, and the fruit growers. This first section describes milk drinkers.

About this [i.e., Christ being a high priest after the order of Melchizedek] *we have much to say which is hard to explain, since you have become dull of hearing. For though by this time you ought to be teachers, you need someone to teach you again the first principles of God's word. You need milk, not solid food; for every one who lives on milk is unskilled in the Word of righteousness, for he is a child. But solid food is for the mature, for those who have their faculties trained by practice to distinguish good from evil.* (Heb. 5:11-14).

Obviously, here is a case of arrested development. Here are people who have been professing Christians for many years. By this time they ought to have been teachers, but they need yet to have someone teach them the very ABC's of the gospel, the Word of Christ. It is a case of retarded maturity. When our daughter was three, it was the undivided opinion of our family that she was the smartest, brightest, and cutest little girl that ever lived. And she said very clever things. We all took great delight in her. But if, at this stage of her life, something had happened; if her body kept growing but her mind stopped and she went on saying the same clever things she was saying, while her body matured and grew into full womanhood, we would not have found delight in what she says. Our joy would have been turned to sorrow; we would have felt great grief at the sight of our dear one suffering from arrested development. This is what this author feels as he writes to these Hebrews.

There is a cloud of threat hanging over these people due to their immaturity. The writer makes three very important and insightful observations about this problem. First, there is the clear suggestion that **age alone does not produce maturity.** It is amazing how many of us think it does. We love this thought of inevitable growth. How often we say, "Just give us time. We have only been Christians for fifteen or twenty years. Perhaps we will yet grow out of these hot tempers, catty tongues and jealous spirits. Just give us time." But time never brings maturity.

I read of a principal in a high school who had an administrative post to fill. He promoted one of his teachers with ten years of teaching experience to the job. When the announcement was made, another teacher in this school came to him terribly upset. She said, "Why did you put that teacher in this position? He has only had ten years of experience and I've had twenty-five years, yet you passed me over in favor of him." And the principal said, "I'm sorry, you're wrong. You haven't had twenty-five years of experience. You have had one year's experience twenty-five times."

That is exactly the situation with these Hebrew Christians. They had been going through the same experience again and again, all the years of their Christian life, but had never grown. Instead of marching forward they were simply marking time. It is the problem with so many of us, is it not? Someone told me the other day that he had analyzed his difficulty and had decided he was suffering from prolonged adolescence, merging into premature senility! It is this process that produces the frequent phenomenon of Christians who come to sit, and soak, and sour. But the writer here makes very clear that age will never cure immaturity.

The second observation he makes is that **immaturity is self-identifying.** It has certain clear marks which provide a simple test that anyone can take to determine whether he belongs in this classification or not. The first mark is an inability to instruct others. Though these have been Christians for years they still cannot help anyone else. They have nothing to say to help another who may be struggling with problems. They cannot even point someone to Christ. There is no ability to help or instruct another. In fact, they themselves can only understand the very simplest doctrinal treatment. They need milk, the writer says, instead of strong meat. They do not understand the "word of righteousness," that is, the divine program which results in right conduct, because they are themselves children and want only milk. That is the first mark of immaturity, an inability to instruct others.

The second mark is an inability to discern good from evil. It is such people who constitute what we may call consecrated blunderers, evangelical crabs, the ones who mean right and think they are doing right but are continually doing the wrong thing, creating problem situations, and difficulties with others. They include the doctrinally undiscerning, that is those who are blown about with every wind of doctrine, who give themselves to the theological fads which come in repetitive cycles. Anyone who has observed the Christian scene for any period of time recognizes there are certain fads which repeat themselves in cycles of interest. These are the doctrinally undiscerning; they go along with every movement that comes.

It includes also the emotionally gullible, that is, those who are moved by some emotional appeal. This is especially true, perhaps, in the realm of missionary appeal. There are those who are affected easily by stories of starving babies, disfigured lepers, and naked savages; who respond to purely emotional stimulation and give their funds only to those organizations or mission boards that make their appeal along these lines. They are uncritical in their evaluation of a work. If it has this emotional content, that is all they look for. Included in this class are those who are frightened by what we might call "religious bogey men"—certain names or personalities that are used as scarecrows because the very use of their name frightens people off from having any part in certain activity. These are the emotionally gullible.

Then this group includes those who are personality followers, those who make much of men, who fasten themselves to one particular outstanding, sparkling personality and read only his books and play his tapes exclusively. I am not speaking against reading books and playing tapes, but I am talking about fastening on to one individual in this respect to the exclusion of others. Those who do this are children, immature, unable to distinguish the activity of the flesh, with its exhibitionism and egotism, from the manifestation of the Spirit. They applaud what God condemns; they resent what God approves.

The third observation the author makes is that **arrested development is a very costly thing.** *About this,* he says, *we have much to say which is hard to explain, since you have become dull of hearing.* "There is so much of the riches of the Melchizedek priesthood of Christ which I want to tell you," he says, "which would make your starved humanity burst into bloom like buds in the spring if you could but grasp it, but you would not get it because you are so dull of hearing." The immature lose so much, and they risk even more. There is a very grave danger threatening those who continue in this condition of prolonged immaturity. He will describe it fully in this next section.

But first we have a brief view of the other side of the picture: the meat eaters, the mature.

Therefore let us leave the elementary doctrines of Christ and go on to maturity, not laying again a foundation of repentance from dead works and of faith toward God, with instruction about ablutions, the laying on of hands, the resurrection of the dead, and eternal judgement. And this we will do if God permits. (Heb. 6:1-3).

It is from this section that we get our title, "Let's get on with it." He is urging these people to graduate from milk to meat, from immature diet to solid food, for, he says, it is this that is the mark of maturity. *Solid food is for the mature.*

In the *Authorized Version* the word for mature is "perfection." *Let us go on to perfection.* I hasten immediately to add, this does not mean sinless perfection. John makes that clear in his first letter, *If we say we have no sin, we deceive ourselves* (we do not fool anyone else, especially our wives, but we deceive ourselves) *and the truth is not in us* (1 John 1:8). No, it is not sinless perfection he is talking about. Paul could write to the Philippians and say, *Let those of us who are mature (perfect) be thus minded* (Phil. 3:15). Yet just three verses before he says, *Not that I have already obtained this or am already perfect* (Phil. 3:12). Notice: there is a maturity, a perfection, which he disowns. That is yet ahead. "I have not reached ultimate perfection, I am not claiming to be sinlessly perfect, I have not yet reached the place where there is nothing at all wrong with me—that lies beyond the Resurrection, that is ahead."

But there is also a maturity which he claims. It is that which in Hebrews has already been called *the rest of God,* a moment-by-moment exercise of faith, a perfect understanding of God's principle of activity, a coming of age, an entering into spiritual manhood. This is what the writer means here. It is not produced by age, as we have already seen, nor by food, for milk will not effect it either, but it is produced by practice. *Those who have their faculties trained by practice to distinguish good from evil* (Heb. 5:14). It is produced by acting on what you believe, stepping out upon it, putting it into practice. That is what brings about maturity.

To reach this requires leaving behind the principles of the gospel, the ABC's, the elementary truths, the familiar ground by which we came into Christian faith. *Not laying again this foundation.* Here is another figure of arrested development. A foundation is laid but nothing is built on it. Instead of building on the foundation, the owner tears it up and lays it again. Then he goes back and lays it yet again. There is nothing but a repetitive laying again and again of the same foundation; it is arrested development. Major Ian Thomas once said to me, "You know, I have discovered an interesting thing about American Christians. They do not usually come to church to learn anything. Whatever they do not yet know themselves they think is heresy. What they want to hear is the same old stuff so they can say, 'Amen, brother,

Amen!' " That is laying the same foundation over and over again.

The foundation is called *the elementary doctrines of Christ* or, in chapter 5, *the first principles of God's word.* The elements of it are listed for us, and they fall into three very interesting groups. There are those doctrinal truths concerning conversion; then teaching concerning church ordinances; and doctrine concerning prophetic matters. This is the milk! This is proper for babies, but is very inadequate for anyone who wishes to go on to maturity, to full growth in the Christian life. He does not mean when he says *leave these* that they are to be forgotten or denied or neglected, but they are no longer to be the chief center of attention. That is the point he is making.

Is it not rather startling that these are often the sole topics on which many ministers dwell? They preach them over and over, and call them "the simple gospel." Because this simple gospel is preached unendingly in our churches, we have Christians who are weak, childish and immature. I have long been convinced that the greatest cause of the weak state of evangelical Christendom today are preachers who never realize that, in preaching what they call the simple gospel, they are feeding their people upon milk. They never get beyond the foundation.

Let's take a closer look at it. The introductory matters concern *repentance from dead works, and faith toward God.* Now those are great themes. They are absolutely essential to the Christian life. But the point the writer makes is, they are only "A" in the alphabet of faith. The teaching about ordinances includes *baptism* (or ablutions) *and laying on of hands.* These are but figures of reality, they are not the reality itself. They are very blessed figures and can be very meaningful, but to get concerned over these shadows, these figures, these pictures, to fight over the mode of baptism or the procedure of ordination is infantile. Dear old Dr. A. T. Pierson used to go about and speak at many churches. When he was in a church that was arguing over the mode of baptism or some such thing, he would say to them, "Quit your baby-talk!" He was quite right. It is overemphasis of these things which leads to the "Mickey Mouse" regulations that are imposed so frequently in many churches.

The last two items, *resurrection and eternal judgment,* obviously have to do with themes of prophecy, eschatology. This would include the time of Christ's return, the question of who the Man of Sin is, where the church will be during the tribulation, etc. All these are important truths, the writer does not deny that, but an over-emphasis of these truths is inclined to puff people up with knowledge instead of to edify in love. "It is time," he says, "to leave these things. You know them, you have been talking about them for too long, now go on, go on, there is much more ahead." *This,* he says, *we will do if God permits.*

With those added three little words he introduces the knottiest, problem passage in Hebrews, if not the whole Bible; a passage which has been a battleground of varying convictions for ages. He changes his figure now and, beginning with verse 4, he brings before us a picture of what I shall call the stillborn.

For it is impossible to restore again to repentance those who have once been enlightened, who have tasted

the heavenly gift, and have become partakers of the Holy Spirit, and have tasted the goodness of the word of God and the powers of the age to come, if they then commit apostasy, since they crucify the Son of God on their own account and hold him up to contempt. For land which has drunk the rain that often falls upon it, and brings forth vegetation useful to those for whose sake it was cultivated, receives a blessing from God. But if it bears thorns and thistles, it is worthless and near to being cursed; its end is to be burned.
(Heb. 6:4-8).

What a sobering passage! There is, first, **the elaboration of an awful possibility.** It is impossible to restore again to repentance these who experience certain Spirit-given blessings, if they shall fall away. The problem of the passage is: how can anyone experience all of this and not be Christian? And if he is Christian, how can he fall away, without any hope of restoration? It is over these issues that the battle was waged hot throughout the Christian ages.

It is important to see that all of this passage hangs upon the three words, *if God permits.* This we will do if God permits. Here is the danger of prolonged immaturity, of remaining in one place all your Christian life. It suggests that you may be one of those whom God will not allow to go further; we have already seen in chapter 3 that God has said of certain ones, *I swore in my wrath, they shall never enter my rest.*

Can we take these expressions here as describing anything other than Spirit-produced, authentic Christian life? Look at them again. *Those who have once been enlightened.* That means to have their eyes opened to their own desperate personal need, to realize they are in a lost world and need a Saviour. That is being enlightened. *Who have tasted the heavenly gift.* What is the heavenly gift? Obviously, it is the gift God gave from heaven. *God so loved the world that he gave his only begotten Son* (John 3:16). These are those who have known a personal encounter with Christ, they have *tasted of the heavenly gift. Become partakers of the Holy Spirit.* That is more than to be influenced by the Holy Spirit, it is to become companions of His, fellow travelers. *They have tasted the goodness of the word of God.* That means to enter into the joy of the promises of God. *And the powers of the age to come,* that is, they have already experienced the miracle of release and deliverance in their life. Yet the sentence stands, *when they commit apostasy* (not "if": there is no if in the original Greek) it is impossible to restore them. Their case is hopeless!

The immediate question here is not, why can they not come back? We will look at that in a moment, but first we must ask, how can they fall away after such a God-honored start as this? I should like to propose an explanation of this which has long haunted me. I would like to raise a question for you to wrestle with which more and more suggests, at least to me, the correct explanation of this phenomenon. We have already noted that Scripture frequently uses the analogy of human birth and growth to explain spiritual birth and growth. We have that even here. The use of milk by children is an analogy drawn from the physical life.

Here is the question I would like to ask. Is it not

possible that we frequently confuse conception with birth? If the spiritual life follows the same pattern as the physical life, we all know that physical life does not begin with birth. It begins with conception. Have we not, perhaps, mistaken conception for birth and therefore have been very confused when certain ones, who seemingly started well, have ended up stillborn? Is there in the spiritual life, as in the natural life, a gestation period before birth when true, Spirit-imparted life can fail and result in a stillbirth? Is there not a time when new Christians are more like embryos, forming little by little in the womb, fed by the faith and vitality of others? We must be careful not to stretch an analogy too far, but perhaps this is what the apostle Paul means when he writes to the Galatians, *My little children, I stand in doubt of you. I am travailing in birth again until Christ be formed in you.* (See Gal. 4:19.)

If this be the case, then the critical moment is not when the Word first meets with faith, for that is conception; that is when the possibility of new life arises. But the critical moment is when the individual is asked to obey the Lord at cost to himself, contrary to his own will and desire. When, in other words, the Lordship of Christ makes demand upon him and comes into conflict with his own desire and purposes, his own plans and program. To put it in terms of what is said of the Lord Jesus in chapter 5, we are called upon to learn obedience at the price of suffering. That is the true moment of birth. *If any man would come after me,* said Jesus, *let him deny himself and take up his cross and follow me* (Matt. 16:24). In grace, the Lord may make this appeal over the course of a number of years. But if obedience to the Lordship of Christ is ultimately refused, this is a stillbirth. The months and even years that may be spent in the enjoyment of conversion, joy was simply Christian life in embryo. The new birth occurs when we first cease from our own works and rest in Jesus Christ. That is when the life of faith begins.

If this step is refused and the decision is made to reject the claims of Christ to Lordship and control, there follows, as Hebrews points out, a hardening, blinding process which, if allowed to continue, may lead such a one to drop out of church and, in effect, to renounce his Christian faith. Though only God knows the true condition of the heart, if that occurs the case, he says, is hopeless. Is this not what the Lord Jesus describes in that parable of the sower in Matthew 13? *Some seed,* he says, *fell on rocky ground* (not gravelly ground, but ground where there was an underlying layer of rock). These are those who receive the Word with joy and endure for awhile, but when persecution or tribulation arises, immediately they fall away.

This brings us to **the explanation for this hopelessness,** this impossibility of return. *It is impossible to restore (them) . . . if they then commit apostasy, since they crucify the Son of God on their own account and hold him up to contempt.* Why is it that God will not permit them to go on in understanding more truth? It is simply because, as far as they are concerned, they are recrucifying Christ. They are repudiating the principle of the cross. They become, as Paul terms it in Philippians, *enemies of the cross of Christ* (Phil. 3:18). From that point on their lives deteriorate and they shame the profession they once made.

Years ago, at the close of World War II, I frequently attended Sunday night meetings in the Church of the Open Door in Los Angeles, sponsored by Youth for Christ. A brilliant young man was the leader of the meetings and a frequent speaker at them. He had a gift for articulation and I heard him give several wonderful messages, simple, clear expositions of the meaning of the cross of Christ, and the offer of life in Christ Jesus. Saturday after Saturday I saw young people come down the aisles to receive Christ in those meetings. But some time after that the young speaker entered a seminary, where he began to drift from his faith. He served for awhile as a national evangelist for his denomination. Finally he quit the ministry entirely and later openly and publicly renounced all faith in Jesus Christ and went back into secular work. Now he lives in a Canadian city and no longer makes any Christian profession.

Is he a case like this? Only God knows the answer, but he could be. John tells us there are certain ones who *went out from us, but they were not of us; for if they had been of us, they would have continued with us; but they went out, that it might be plain that they all are not of us* (1 John 2:19). There is a conversion of the head that never reaches the heart.

On Palm Sunday we celebrate the Lord's triumphal entry into Jerusalem. I doubt if He would ever have called it a triumphal entry. He probably would have referred to it as a day of sorrows. That was the day when He left the donkey's back to go into the Temple and, for the second time in His ministry, clean out the money-changers and the filth that had accumulated in His Father's house. It was then that He stopped the offerings of Israel and would not permit any man to offer sacrifice in the Temple. Then He went up on the Mount of Olives and, looking out over the city, His heart broke in yearning over that wretched city, and He cried out those unforgettable words, *O Jerusalem, Jerusalem, killing the prophets and stoning those who are sent to you! How often would I have gathered your children together as a hen gathers her brood under her wings, and you would not!* (Matt. 23:37). The tears coursing down His face, He wept for the city. One week later He was nailed to a cross outside that very city's gates. Where was the multitude that greeted Him when He came on the triumphal entry? Oh, they were there, but they were the ones who were now crying out, *Crucify Him, crucify Him! He said He was the Son of God, let Him save Himself!*

We have another picture of this apostasy in the case of Judas who for three years accompanied the Lord in His ministry, was sent out with the Twelve and given power to heal, to cast out demons, to preach the gospel. But at the end, despite the manifestations of Spirit-given power, there was no faith and he turned and went out into the dark night of betrayal.

The last word on this is **the illustration of its reality,** the account of the two plots of land which have drunk in the rain. It is a very simple illustration, and it parallels the parable of the sower that our Lord told. There were two plots of ground, side by side, both containing good seed. The rain falls on each. One brings forth fruit but on the other the good seed sprouts but because it has no root, some of it dies. The thorns and thistles take over and choke out the rest. The rain pictures the Spirit-given blessings of verses 4 and 5. What good does more rain do on ground like that? It can only mean more thorns and thistles. This is why God will not permit someone to go on in truth until they cease their own works and depend on His. It is the principle of faith that alone will receive anything from God. The whole of Scripture testifies to it. For those who refuse to act on that, the end is to be burned.

Now the final figure, the fruit growers.

Though we speak thus, yet in your case, beloved, we feel sure of better things that belong to salvation. For God is not so unjust as to overlook your work and the love which you showed for his sake in serving the saints, as you still do. And we desire each one of you to show the same earnestness in realizing the full assurance of hope until the end, so that you may not be sluggish, but imitators of those who through faith and patience inherit the promises.
(Heb. 6:9-12).

There were certain evidences that convinced the writer of this letter that the case was not one of embryo Christians being threatened with stillbirth. There had been a true birth, he thinks, for he has seen unmistakable evidence of love and concern for others, expressed in deeds of compassion. Not simply words but deeds, ministry, help to others. This is the test the Lord has said He will look for. *As you did it to one of the least of these my brethren,* [unconsciously, unknowingly, out of a heart filled with concern for me] *you did it to me* (Matt. 25:40).

But as the writer thinks of these dear Hebrew Christians, he says, "Your life is so weak and struggling. I am so anxious that you manifest an earnest, whole-souled, fervent hunger to learn and to act and to stay with it!" That is the proven pattern of victory. That is what those in the past have done, those who *by faith and patience inherit the promises.* The result will be the full assurance of hope. That is his theme for the next section.

Do you live in uncertainty about your Christian faith? Are you constantly aware of a vague sense of guilt and questioning? Do you have times of real, troubling doubt? Are you still talking baby-talk and drinking the milk of elementary things? The word of the Holy Spirit from this great passage is, "Wake up! Get serious! Give full attention to this." Nothing will ever be more important. Begin to practice what you know, put it to work. And as you do, you will discover that full assurance of hope that makes others stop and look. Our age, our poor, restless, troubled, bedeviled age, is hungering for the manifestation, the visible evidence, of the sons of God.

"As before, Lord, these words have searched us, have found us out, have made us to see ourselves. We thank You for that. We do not want to live behind unreal facades, we do not want to be self-deceived. We thank You for telling us the truth even though it may hurt, for we know that it is always to the end that we may be healed. Grant that this may be true in the individual ministry of the Spirit to each life.
In Christ's name,
Amen."

6

dealing with doubt

Our last study in Hebrews 6 revealed a very sobering possibility. We may look back upon a "conversion experience" accompanied by joy, release, and forgiveness. It may have been twenty or thirty years ago. But the opening verses of chapter 6 make very clear that if there is no permanent change in our life today as a result of that conversion experience, then we may have only been kidding ourselves. We are not Christians. Despite the religious activities we may have faithfully performed in the intervening years, if we are still the same persons in our dispositions and attitudes, our reactions to other people, then are we truly Christians. We are still without life—dead!

The unmistakable sign of true Christian life is the existence of a love that desires to help others, that seeks to minister to others at cost to self. If that love is present, even in some small degree, it is proof that we are truly Christians. (See John 15:12-17.) But we can have even that without any sense of assurance, of security in this relationship. It is very possible, therefore, to be a Christian and still be troubled with doubts, fears, and uncertainties about our relationship to Christ.

I once received a letter from a Christian boy in the service who was tormented with doubts about his faith. He expressed his concern very openly. He said, in part, "I think I've lost my faith in the power of prayer. It seems like I have asked so many things in Christ's name that weren't answered. I get the skeptical feeling that it would have happened one way or the other whether I asked or not. If it comes out the way you ask, then you say, 'My prayer was answered'; if it doesn't, you say, 'God chose not to answer it this way' or 'He'll answer it later if I keep praying,' etc. I haven't by any means rejected Christianity. But I can't, no matter how much I want to, give myself wholeheartedly to a way of life I am so uncertain about. But it's really rough, riding on the fence."

I appreciate the honesty of that letter. There may be many of us who feel the same way, who are not honest enough to say so. I would like to let this climate of doubt, expressed by that letter so simply and forthrightly, be the launching pad for the rocket of faith (always the answer to doubt), which this passage of Hebrews will bring before us. The writer cites the example of Abraham, one of the great rocket launchers of all history, the man called in the New Testament, "the father of the faithful." To exercise the kind of faith Abraham exercised is to become a child of Abraham, and an heir of his promises. This incident from the life of Abraham will show us what makes faith strong. Here we learn the reason for faith, the ground of our hope.

For when God made a promise to Abraham, since he had no one greater by whom to swear, he swore by himself, saying, "Surely I will bless you and multiply you." And thus Abraham, having patiently endured, obtained the promise. Men indeed swear by a greater than themselves, and in all their disputes an oath is final for confirmation. So when God desired to show more convincingly to the heirs of the promise the unchangeable character of his purpose, he interposed with an oath, so that through two unchangeable things, in which it is impossible that God should prove false, we who have fled for refuge might have strong encouragement to seize the hope set before us. We have this as a sure and steadfast anchor of the soul, a hope that enters into the inner shrine behind the curtain, where Jesus has gone as a forerunner on our behalf, having become a high priest for ever after the order of Melchizedek.
(Heb. 6:13-20).

Genesis records that God appeared to Abraham and made him a promise: *In thy seed shall all the nations of the earth be blessed*[1] (Gen. 22:18). The immediate seed was Isaac, born of Abraham's old age; but the ultimate Seed is Christ. It is through faith in Jesus Christ that this promise is fulfilled, and all the peoples of the earth are blessed in Abraham. This promise was later confirmed by an oath, God swearing by Himself that He would fulfill what He had said. The writer is simply pointing out that Abraham believed God's promise and His oath.

Why did he believe it? Not because he immediately saw it fulfilled! There were twenty-five long, weary years before Isaac was born, and in the meantime, Abraham and his wife Sarah were growing older and had passed the time of life when it was possible to have children. Still the promise was unfulfilled. Abraham did not believe it because he saw immediate results. Nor did he believe because he was doing his best to accomplish it. There was one occasion when he began to waver in faith and thought he had to help God out. He concocted an ingenious scheme to fulfill the promise of God, and the result was the birth of Ishmael who became a thorn in the side of Israel from that day to this.

Then why did Abraham believe God's promise? Let us read from Paul's letter to the Romans in chapter 4, where he writes of Abraham:

He did not weaken in faith when he considered his own body, which was as good as dead because he was about a hundred years old, or when he considered the barrenness of Sarah's womb. No distrust made him waver concerning the promise of God, but he grew strong in his faith as he gave glory to God, fully convinced that God was able to do what he had promised (Rom. 4:19-21).

God was able. Abraham's faith rested on the character of God. That is always where faith must rest. As the writer points out, this is also true among men. A man's word is no better than his character. Even if you get a man to sign a contract or agreement, that agreement is no more than a scrap of paper if the man who signed it does not intend to fulfill it. It is no better than the man who makes it. Even in our courts of law and affairs of business this is true. All faith ultimately rests on character.

Abraham believed that God told the truth about Himself, that God was true to His own character which He had expressed in two separate ways. First, the promise, and second, the oath by which He swore to fulfill that promise. Without seeing any results for twenty-five years, Abraham hung on to the character of God. He never said to himself during that time, "I've tried it and it doesn't work," or "I've got to convince myself that this is true, even though I secretly believe that it is not." He said, "The God I know exists is the kind of a God who will do what He says He'll do." For twenty-five years Abraham hung on to that promise. And he won!

Now I come back for a moment to my friend's letter. He raises a question about prayer. He says, "I've tried prayer but it doesn't seem to work." It seems to me that is putting things the wrong way. That is really repeating the common myth of our day, "seeing is believing." Have you ever said that? "If I see it then I'll believe it." No greater lie was ever foisted upon the human race by the father of lies than this, that seeing is believing. We are often convinced that is the way to come to the knowledge of truth, but the truth is, the man who sees no longer needs to believe. Faith is not sight, nor sight faith.

You ask me why I believe in prayer? Well, not because I have tried it and it has worked. I believe in prayer because Jesus Christ says that prayer is the secret of life and I believe Him. Jesus Christ says that man must either pray or faint, one or the other, that he either finds the keystone to life in prayer or, lacking it, life begins to come apart at the seams. Because it is Jesus Christ who says this, I believe

Him and therefore I pray and find it works. For it *is* the secret, He has been telling the truth. The proof of prayer does not come from my experience; that is simply the demonstration of what I have already believed, but I believe it because of who said it. Believing, therefore, is seeing. That is the truth.

This is true of many levels of life. Albert Einstein did not come to the knowledge of relativity by performing a series of experiments which ultimately convinced him that relativity was true. He gradually "saw" the concept of relativity and, convinced in his own mind that this was the secret of the physical universe, he performed experiments that he might demonstrate it to others. This is the way of truth. Believing is seeing.

This, therefore, is the secret of faith; it rests on the character of Jesus Christ. Either He is telling us the truth and we can trust what this One, who is like no one else in human history, says to us, or we must reject Him and repudiate Him as a self-deceived imposter who attempted to foist some crude and foolish ideas upon the human race. That is where faith rests. From that ground everything else must follow.

We have this as a sure and steadfast anchor of the soul, a hope that enters into the inner shrine behind the curtain, where Jesus has gone as a forerunner on our behalf.
(Heb. 6:19,20).

It is in the person of Christ that all Christian faith rests, at last. He is our forerunner. Not only has He made promises but He has Himself demonstrated them. What has happened to Him is what will happen to us. Now if this be true, then our faith will be strengthened as we see more clearly the character of the One with whom we have to deal. This is why the author moves immediately to the matter of the high priesthood of Melchizedek.

Again and again in this letter he has used this phrase, a high *priest for ever after the order of Melchizedek.* The sheer repetition of it indicates there is something very vital hidden here. Now we shall see what that is. In this next section, Hebrews 7:1-26, we have a portrait of our helper. The incident upon which it is based comes again from Abraham's life, recorded in the fourteenth chapter of Genesis, the story of Abraham and Melchizedek. As Abraham was returning from battle with the five kings a stranger met him and blessed him, and Abraham gave tithes to this man. Melchizedek steps suddenly out of the shadows of history, to appear on the stage of Scripture. Perhaps we shall be greatly helped to understand if we view this incident as a movie depicting the life of Christ.

For this Melchizedek, king of Salem, priest of the most high God, met Abraham returning from the slaughter of the kings and blessed him; and to him Abraham apportioned a tenth part of everything. He is first, by translation of his name, king of righteousness, and then he is also king of Salem, that is, king of peace. He is without father or mother or genealogy, and has neither beginning of days nor end of life, but resembling the Son of God he continues a priest forever (Heb. 7:1-3).

This is like a motion picture in which a well-known star plays the part of a historical character, as a few years ago Raymond Massey played the part of Abraham Lincoln. Throughout that movie you did not see Raymond Massey, but you saw Abraham Lincoln, for within the scope of a movie the star is no longer himself, but is for all practical purposes the very character whose role he is interpreting. This account in Genesis is that kind of a scene. Here is an ordinary man named Melchizedek, a priest of the true God, who lived in the village of Salem (later known as Jerusalem) and who met Abraham returning from battle. For the moment he is fulfilling a role which beautifully pictures the ministry of Jesus Christ to us today. In passing let me add this: Hollywood could never duplicate this, for in their movies they must of necessity have the star play the part of a man of the past, but when God directs a movie, He has His man play the part of the Man of the future!

Now let us look more carefully at this passage to see the meaning of this ministry of Christ's, first **by comparison** with Melchizedek. There is a word of reciprocity in these first two verses. Melchizedek met Abraham and gave to him bread and wine which are the symbols of life and strength, the very things that we partake of when we come to the Lord's table. Abraham, in turn, gave tithes of everything he possessed to Melchizedek.

Now the tithe, or tenth, is always the mark of ownership. To pay a tenth is to indicate that God owns the whole. In symbol, therefore, Abraham was saying to Melchizedek, "The One whom you depict has the right of ownership over everything in my life." And in this movie of the ministry of Jesus Christ we see enacted a very important principle. Abraham and Melchizedek become available to each other. The provision of strength from Melchizedek exactly equaled the degree of commitment on the part of Abraham. This is what the New Testament says to us. You may exercise dominion to the same degree you are prepared to submit to the dominion of Jesus Christ in your own heart. You can fulfill your God-given right as man to be king over all you survey, to the same degree you are prepared to recognize the Kingship of Jesus Christ in your own life. You can have as much of Christ as, in turn, you are ready to permit Him to have of you!

Then there is a word of authority here! *He is first, by translation of his name, king of righteousness, and then he is also king of Salem, that is, king of peace.* What is it that Jesus Christ can give you today? What does His present ministry make possible in your life right now? He can give you only what He is, that is all. It takes Christ to be a Christian! We need what He is in order to be what He was, and what He is is revealed in His names. He is, first of all, *king of righteousness;* that is, He is the One who has the secret of right conduct, the principle, the divine program which results in proper behavior. He is the king of that, He controls it. He is also the king of peace. May I use the equivalent modern term for that phrase? Mental health! He is the king of mental health, the king of peace. He holds in His hand the secret of rest, of inner calm, of that adequacy within that gives poise, power and purpose to human life. This is so desperately being sought today.

Then there is a word of continuity here. *He is without father or mother or genealogy, and has neither beginning of days nor end of life, but resembling the Son of God he continues a priest forever.* In the movie of Melchizedek that we are looking at here, all this verse means is that there is no mention made of Melchizedek's ancestry, his pedigree or any record of his birth or death. He was a perfectly normal man, all these things were true of him, but the silence of the record is taken as an illustration of the eternal, changeless, unending priesthood of Jesus Christ. Christ is available twenty-four hours a day, seven days a week, fifty-two weeks a year, throughout every year of a whole lifetime.

Someone said to me, "How much time do you spend with the Lord each day?"

I looked at him and said, "Twenty-four hours. How much time do you?"

And he said, "Oh, no, what I mean is, how much time do you have for your quiet time every morning, your time with the Lord?"

"Well," I said, "I do try to have a quiet time every morning. Sometimes I miss, but that doesn't mean I haven't had time with the Lord. I have discovered from the New Testament that I have time with Him twenty-four hours a day. I am never out of His presence, I am never shut off from His resources, I am never separated from His wisdom or His peace or His truth."

That is what the Melchizedek priesthood means and what the world is so mightily hungering after today.

Now let us take another look at this from the

negative point of view. In the next section we see the ministry of Jesus **by contrast** with the Levitical priesthood. Here is indicated the incompleteness and weakness of every source of help outside of Christ. As we sing in the old hymn, "All other ground is sinking sand."

First it is evident that Christ is superior to the Jewish priesthood. We shall move quickly here for it is not necessary to spend much time in exposition.

See how great he (Melchizedek) *is! Abraham the patriarch gave him a tithe of the spoils. And those descendants of Levi who receive the priestly office have a commandment in the law to take tithes from the people, that is, from their brethren, though these also are descended from Abraham. But this man who has not their genealogy received tithes from Abraham and blessed him who had the promises. It is beyond dispute that the inferior is blessed by the superior. Here* (i.e., in the Levitical priesthood) *tithes are received by mortal men; there* (in the Melchizedek priesthood), *by one of whom it is testified that he lives. One might even say that Levi himself, who receives tithes, paid tithes through Abraham, for he was still in the loins of his ancestor when Melchizedek met him.*
(Heb. 7:4-10).

We have already seen in this letter that the job of a priest is to make one fit for life, able to cope. May I again substitute a modern term for the word "priest," one which perhaps we will understand a bit better? The modern equivalent of the priest is the psychotherapist! This is his job, is it not, to help make you fit for living? Not only fit to live but fit to be lived with! The Levitical priests of the old order were an ancient type of psychotherapists. They offered help to men and women in the problems of living. Read the Old Testament insightfully and you will see that is exactly the function they fulfilled. They were there to help others with the problems of guilt, stress, confusion and uncertainty.

Now the argument of the writer here is very simple. He points out that these Levitical priests derived their authority by descent from Abraham. Therefore they could never offer any greater help than Abraham could have offered. But Abraham acknowledged the supremacy of Melchizedek by paying tithes to him. Therefore, the help available in the Levitical priests was, by comparison, incomplete, secondary, limited and temporary. These priests were limited by the humanity of Abraham, just as any psychiatrist or psychologist today is limited by his own humanity. He can only go so far. The help he gives may be very real. Let us not confuse the issue or refuse to face facts. Psychiatrists and psychologists can often give much real help, but only to a degree, only within a limit, only so far. That is the argument of the writer here.

Just how far is revealed in this next section of Hebrews, where we learn that the ministry of Jesus Christ supersedes the law.

Now if perfection had been attainable through the Levitical priesthood (for under it the people received the law), what further need would there have been for another priest to arise after the order of Melchizedek,

rather than one named after the order of Aaron? For when there is a change in the priesthood, there is necessarily a change in the law as well. For the one of whom these things are spoken (i.e., Christ) *belonged to another tribe, from which no one has ever served at the altar. For it is evident that our Lord was descended from Judah, and in connection with that tribe Moses said nothing about priests. This becomes even more evident when another priest arises in the likeness of Melchizedek, who has become a priest, not according to a legal requirement concerning bodily descent but by the power of an indestructible life. For it is witnessed of him, "Thou art a priest forever, after the order of Melchizedek." On the one hand, a former commandment is set aside because of its weakness and uselessness (for the law made nothing perfect); on the other hand, a better hope is introduced, through which we draw near to God.*
(Heb. 7:11-19).

One thing clearly marked the fact that the old priesthood was no longer acceptable as help for men. It was the appearance of a new priest with a different address and a different ancestry. And if the old priesthood went, the law had to go, too. That is the argument here. This new priest had a quite different address; He came from the tribe of Judah instead of the tribe of Levi. Judah was not a priestly tribe at all, but a kingly tribe. The new priest was a king. Obviously, some change has been made. If God recognizes Christ as a priest, then there has been a change made, the law which was part of the old priesthood has been set aside.

Also, the new priest has a different ancestry. It was not necessary for Him to trace His genealogy back to Abraham. No, as a priest He has no genealogy. He ministers in the power of an endless life. He had no beginning, no ending, but continues forever. Therefore the law, which is only temporary, must go. It had an inherent weakness in that it could not supply what the flesh in its frailty lacked. Every priest, every psychiatrist, every counselor, every behavior-consultant, whether he realizes it or not, is continually working with the law. How? By seeking to relate people to reality. That is basically what the law is, the revelation of reality. It is the way things are. Any knowledgeable psychologist or psychiatrist tries to help the people who come to him to see things as they are. That is their entire ministry. There is nothing else they can do. But even that is sometimes a very difficult help to render.

Dr. Henry Brandt, the well-known Christian psychologist, was speaking to a number of us in a private meeting. He referred to James, chapter 3, verse 14, *But if ye have bitter envying and strife in your hearts, glory not, and lie not against the truth.*[1] Dr. Brandt said this is very illuminating for it reveals what we usually do when we have strife, envy, bitter jealousy or selfish ambition in our hearts. We cover it over and glory, actually boast, in our ability to pretend that we do not have it there. Thus we lie against the truth.

Have you ever said to someone, "You know, I felt like telling that fellow off, but I didn't say a word. I smiled sweetly and didn't say a word. But it burns me up to have him do a thing like that." Do you know what is the worst thing about that? We think it is Christian! We think we have done the Christian thing because we have covered up our enmity and hidden it away, playacting and pretending it was not there. That, we think, is spiritual. But James goes on to point out that it comes from a low source: *This wisdom descendeth not from above, but is earthly, sensual, devilish*[1] (Jas. 4:15).

Dr. Brandt says that "sensual" means "pleasurable." The problem, we discover when someone tries to help us, is that we like to be bitter. It is pleasurable to feel this way toward somebody. We like to be angry and mull things over in our minds, to bear a grudge and nurse a spirit of hatred against someone. We like it, we do not want to give it up, it is pleasurable. The job of any psychiatrist or psychologist, Christian or otherwise, is simply to help us to see that we are hiding the truth from ourselves, deceiving ourselves. But that is as far as they can go.

Once self-discovery comes, then what? Well, under the old order a man would take a sacrifice to the priest and the priest would offer it; and thus, for the moment at least, remove the guilt of the act. Though the problem remained, the guilt from it was removed. That is what the modern priest does. A psychiatrist attempts to dispel guilt by helping his client see his problem in a different light. Or, if he is a Christian psychologist or psychiatrist, to help him to see that God has already forgiven him in Christ and thus to remove his guilt feelings. But the basic problem essentially remains, if resolving guilt is all that is done. The psychiatrist may rearrange the problem so it does not grate so strongly upon others, but basically the problem remains. As C. S. Lewis puts it, "No clever arrangement of bad eggs will ever make a good omelet."

Self-discovery is the end of the line as far as the human psychiatrist, counselor, priest, or what-have-you, can go. But what lies beyond that? Well, if you do not go any further, eventually despair! This is what Paul reflects in Romans 7, *I do not do the good I want, but the evil I do not want is what I do. . . . Wretched man that I am! Who will deliver me from this body of death?* (Rom. 7:19,24). Well, that is where this word of Hebrews comes in. There is a Priest who can go further. There is a wisdom, James says, which is from above, to be received as a gift, which is pure, peaceable, gentle, easy to be intreated, without partiality, without hypocrisy, waiting to be received. *What the law could not do, in that it was weak through the flesh, God sending his own Son in the likeness of sinful flesh, and for sin, condemned sin in the flesh: that the righteousness of the law might be fulfilled in us, who walk not after the flesh, but after the Spirit*[1] (Rom. 8:3,4). That which is worthless, weak, and useless has been set aside and a new hope introduced which brings us near to God.

Now return to the text for one more contrast. Not only is the ministry of Jesus superior in greatness to the priesthood of old, and superseding the incompleteness, the temporariness of the law, but in His person He Himself surpasses all that any human priest can do.

And it (i.e., the Melchizedek priesthood) *was not without an oath. Those who formerly became priests took their office without an oath, but this one was addressed with an oath, "The Lord has sworn and will not change his mind 'Thou art a priest forever.' " This makes Jesus the surety of a better covenant. The former priests were many in number, because they were prevented by death from continuing in office; but he holds his priesthood permanently, because he continues forever. Consequently he is able for all time to save those who draw near to God through him, since he always lives to make intercession for them. For it was fitting that we should have such a high priest, holy, blameless, unstained, separated from sinners, exalted above the heavens.* (Heb. 7:20-26).

Note the argument. In the old order the priest never took an oath because the law was a temporary measure. It was never the ultimate divine intention for the control of men. Never. It was necessary, but it was never the permanent divine intention. But in Christ the permanent program has come, therefore His ministry was confirmed with an oath. God says thereby, "I will never change my mind. You will never be able to find any other program that works. Never. You will not find in all the writings of men, in all the thinking of the world, another way of achieving proper human behavior. I will never change my mind." Because this is permanent, there is no shutdown!

Further, the old priests inevitably died and the help they offered could therefore suddenly terminate. A lady said to me some time ago, "I don't know what I'm going to do. My psychiatrist is moving away and I'm simply lost without him." But here is a psychiatrist who never dies, who never moves away, who is never off duty. Therefore, with Him there is no breakdown! He can save to the uttermost. Is that not good news? As someone has well put it, "From the guttermost to the uttermost." No wonder then the writer says in verse 26, "It was fitting that we should have such a high priest." Very fitting, is it not? He is just made for us in our pressure-filled, hectic, highly mobile, tension-torn days. Someone has put it in a beautiful acrostic with the name of Jesus; J-E-S-U-S "Just Exactly Suits Us Sinners".

Now what is the key that releases this ministry to us? It is written all through Hebrews–faith. Not belief! I did not say belief; we all believe this, but only a few are acting upon it, exercising faith. One night at a meeting of the board of elders of our church three men shared together with us their experiences in witnessing. They told of the delight and surprise that was theirs, the joy that was in their heart, as they actually found that people all around them were eager to talk about the things of Christ. After they had finished, two other men spoke up on their own and told about their failures. They confessed that they wanted to do this but they simply had not–could not, they thought! Now, if you had given an examination to all the men of that board on the doctrine of witnessing, they would have all passed. There was not a man there who did not believe that the Holy Spirit is at work awakening hunger in hearts, that God is able to save, that there are those ready to be talked to, and that there is joy in witnessing. All would have passed. But there were only three who had exercised faith! For faith is a venture, faith is putting your foot out on a principle, faith is attempting it, trying it. Those three men could say that every word they had believed was true. So unless we make continual demands upon Christ's love and power, how else will we ever learn that we can never touch bottom?

"We remember, Lord Jesus, how many times you said to Your disciples, 'O ye of little faith.' We hear these words again in our own hearts, Lord. Grant to us that we may have the courage to believe and to step out upon what we believe. Stir us up, Lord. Grant to us this ability to act on what we know.
In Your name,
Amen."

7

the new constitution

The other day a little boy came home from Sunday School and his mother asked, "How was the Sunday School class?"

He said, "Oh, we had a new teacher, and guess who it was?"

His mother said, "Who was it?"

He said, "It was Jesus' grandmother!"

She said, "Why, what made you think that?"

He answered, "Well, all she did was show us pictures of Jesus and tell us stories about Him."

There is something of that flavor about the book of Hebrews. The author of Hebrews simply cannot take his eyes off Christ. He is writing to buffeted, often baffled, confused, harassed, and persecuted Christians of that first century, who were tempted to coldness and dullness because of the glamour of the false all around them. We heard him say in our last study together in the seventh chapter, *It was fitting that we should have such a high priest, holy, blameless, unstained, separated from sinners, exalted above the heavens* (Heb. 7:26).

Christ was just what they needed! And because this is Scripture and is thus written for all people of God in all ages, it is also true that He is just exactly what we need in these baffling, pressure-filled, bewildering days of the twentieth century.

Now, between verses 26 and 27 of chapter 7, there is a major division in the letter. I have a continual quarrel with whoever put the chapter divisions in our Bible. They are seldom in the right place, from my point of view. They miss it by two verses this time. Between these two verses the writer turns from his discussion of the person of Jesus Christ, to that which occupies the next chapters, His work, His sacrifice. The next three chapters focus on the great altar of the cross and the bleeding sacrifice that hung there. You will never understand Jesus Christ except in connection with His cross, and you will never understand the cross apart from the person of Christ. These are indivisibly united.

In chapter 8 we shall see that this transforming event opened up for Christ a new dimension of ministry, and results for us in a new arrangement for living. What do I mean when I say "a new dimension of ministry"? The answer is found in the last two verses of chapter 7, and the first five verses of chapter 8. There is first, **a perfect sacrifice.**

He has no need, like those high priests, to offer sacrifices daily, first for his own sins and then for those of the people; he did this once for all when he offered

up himself. Indeed, the law appoints men in their weakness as high priests, but the word of the oath, which came later than the law, appoints a Son who has been made perfect forever.
(Heb. 7:27,28).

Join two phrases of that passage together to get the main thought: *he offered up himself . . . and was made perfect.* As a priest, Jesus Christ could find no unblemished sacrifice that He could offer except Himself, so He offered Himself. As a sacrifice, there was found no other priest worthy of offering such a sacrifice, so Christ became both Priest and Victim.

On Good Friday many of us gather to listen to the words of Christ from the cross. In uttering the first three words from the cross, Jesus is a priest. *Father, forgive them; for they know not what they do* (Luke 23:34). He is interceding for the bloody murderers who have nailed Him to this tree. Then He turns to the thief at His side and says, *Today you will be with me in Paradise* (Luke 23:43). He is ministering grace to this redhanded revolutionary who readily admitted his need. Then to His mother and the disciple John, who were standing at the foot of the cross, He said, *Woman, behold, your son! . . . Behold, your mother!* (John 19:26,27). He is still a priest ministering comfort to their hearts, giving one to the other to meet the need of life.

But at this moment a change occurred. The sun was hidden and a strange, unaccountable darkness fell across the face of the land for three hours. The first word from the cross, out of the midst of that darkness, is the terrible cry of dereliction, "Immanuel's orphaned cry." *My God, my God, why hast thou forsaken me?* (Matt. 27:46). Now He is no longer a priest; He is the victim, offered as a sacrifice on the altar of the cross. Then from the midst of that hot hell of pain and even more excruciating anguish of spirit, come the words, *I thirst* (John 19:28). This is followed by the last two cries from the cross, when with a loud voice at the end of the three hours, He shouted, *It is finished* (John 19:30). And then, *Father, into thy hands I commit my spirit!* (Luke 23:46). Immediately, He gave up the ghost. In those last words He is still a sacrifice, having completed the work that the Father gave Him to do.

If you will join two more phrases of this passage together you will get the complete thought of the writer here. Not only did Christ offer up Himself as the perfect sacrifice, but He did it *once for all . . . forever.* That means the cross is a timeless event. It is not simply a historic occurrence that we may look back upon and study as we would the Battle of Waterloo or Gettysburg. It is an intrusion of eternity into time. It is timeless. It is as though it is going on forever and had been going on since the foundation of the world. It is therefore eternally contemporary. Christians are quite accurate when they speak of the cross as "a contemporary experience."

Every age can know for itself the meaning of this cross. It reaches back to cover all history so that it can be said that Jesus is "the Lamb slain from the foundation of the world." Thus all those of the Old Testament who had not yet known of the historic presentation of Christ could be saved, just as we are saved today, for the cross reached backward into time as well as forward. The cross of Jesus Christ, from God's point of view, is the central act of history. Everything flows from that. From that great event all hope is flowing, all light is flaming, it is to it that all events must look for meaning.

Now this is what I mean when I say that Christ ministers in a new dimension, an eternal dimension, performing a contemporary act that is always meaningful. This gives point to what the author says next: the results of this perfect sacrifice are being continually ministered to us **in the proper sanctuary.**

Now the point in what we are saying is this: we have such a high priest, one who is seated at the right hand of the throne of the Majesty in heaven, a minister in the sanctuary and the true tent which is set up not by man but by the Lord. For every high priest is appointed to offer gifts and sacrifices; hence it is necessary for this priest also to have something to offer. Now if he were on earth, he would not be a priest at all, since there are priests who offer gifts according to the law. They serve a copy and shadow of the heavenly sanctuary; for when Moses was about to erect the tent [*the Tabernacle*], *he was instructed by God, saying, "See that you make everything according to the pattern which was shown you on the mountain"* (Heb. 8:1-5).

As the writer says, the point of emphasis in what he has been saying is not duration but location! The question is! Where is this kind of ministry of Jesus Christ available? Where do you find it? He answers that it comes from the risen Christ who is at the right hand of the throne of the Majesty in heaven, a minister of the true sanctuary which God made and not man. Now if the picture you get from that is that we are poor struggling mortals left here on planet Earth, and Christ is somewhere out in space in heaven, "out there," then you miss the entire point. I confess that for many years this was the concept I held and therefore I greatly missed the whole point and blessing of what the writer says.

It is true, of course, that Jesus Christ is in heaven, but where is heaven? Well, heaven is not "out there" somewhere, remote in space. It is not some spatial location which can be pinpointed on some other planet in some distant galaxy in the great reaches of space. Heaven is within. Heaven is this new dimension which is as present on earth as it is anywhere else. *The kingdom of God (heaven),* Jesus said, *is within you*[1] (Luke 17:21). It will help us to understand this if we look at what he says about the pattern, for the Tabernacle was a pattern of this.

We are told that Moses built the Tabernacle according to a pattern which was shown him when he ascended Mount Sinai to receive the Law from the hands of God. He was given specific instructions: "See that you make everything according to the pattern which was shown you on the mountain." When the Tabernacle took form and shape under the direction of Moses, it was a copy of something else that Moses had already seen.

A copy of what? The Tabernacle, you remember, was built in three parts. There was a great outer court into which the people could come, but no Gentiles. There was a structure in the center of this court divided into two sections. One part was called the Holy Place where were located certain articles of furniture. Into that Holy Place only the priests and the Levites could enter. The third part of the Tabernacle was the rear section of this structure, called the holy of holies, containing in it nothing but the Ark of the Covenant of God, where dwelt the Shekinah glory, the glowing light that indicated the presence of God. Into that holy of holies, hidden behind the veil, entrance was prohibited to all upon pain of death, with the exception of the high priest who could enter once a year and then only under the most rigid requirements involving the slaying of a sacrifice and the bearing in of a basin of blood.

All this was but a pattern, a shadow, a copy of the truth. The fascinating thing is that this is exactly the structure of the universe! We live in a universe made on three levels. There is, first of all, the world of matter, the world of things, material or physical structure that we can touch, sense, see, taste, and smell. There is a great and varied area for discovery and exploration in this world. Science works in this field. Then there is the world of mind, the world of ideas, of emotions, of the arts, of knowledge, and the interchange of human thought. It, too, is a rich world, inviting voyages of discovery. Beyond this is the world of spirit, a world of vast mystery to us. It is a world in which are hidden the secrets of life and light and love; the keys to living are all in that world of the spirit. That is why man has such a difficult time, for the problems that develop in the worlds of matter and of mind have their solution in the world of spirit. But into that world we cannot enter–no man can. It is a world separated from us, shut away from us. We have no way of access to it in ourselves.

Now Moses was shown all this. He saw the invisible realities of the nature of God, the structure of the universe and man's need for a Mediator, a way of access, a way of entrance into this world where all the secrets of life are hidden. Man, in the uniqueness of his nature and structure, is designed to live in all three of these worlds, ultimately. It is God's intention that man should have access to the inner world. We have no difficulty now with the worlds of mind and matter. We find our bodies to be keenly and wonderfully adapted to the world of matter. We can touch this world, taste it, sense it, feel it, examine it, explore it, analyze it, take it apart and put it together again, rearrange it. We are also adapted to enter the world of mind. We can explore it, we can weigh ideas, we can analyze them, we can entertain the various thoughts of men and we find wonderful delight in doing this. We can enjoy music and beauty of structure and form. But into the world of spirit we cannot enter. There is only One who can enter that realm, that Holy of Holies–the High Priest!

By means of a cross, our High Priest, the only High Priest man will ever have, entered into the Holy of Holies. He broke through into the realm of the spirit so that He is able to set man free in the area where He has been held in greatest bondage. Through Him we can enter into this wonderful realm where the secrets of life are held. The cross of Jesus is the gateway into the realm of the spirit, and we penetrate into this secret place of our own being only as we do so through Jesus Christ. The cross is made for the whole man, therefore the cross can be understood on three levels of life.

There is the understanding of the cross on the physical level: its pain, its anguish, the awful thirst of it. There is an understanding of the cross on the emotional level. It is a moving experience to contemplate what occurs in the minds and hearts of those connected with the cross, and especially in the Saviour's mind. But the real meaning of the cross never comes to us except as we move into the realm of the spirit, where we are entirely dependent on revelation. Our minds or emotions are incapable of explaining it on this level. We have to accept what God says it means. But on that level we discover there is marvelous meaning and insight on life granted to us in the cross. In the next section the writer begins to unfold to us the results of this sacrifice. The first part reveals the provision, in the cross, of a new arrangement for living.

If there is a new arrangement, that suggests of course that there must have been an old arrangement. For a brief instant we must look at **the predicted failure** of the law, the old arrangement.

But as it is, Christ has obtained a ministry which is as much more excellent than the old as the covenant he mediates is better, since it is enacted on better promises. For if that first covenant had been faultless, there would have been no occasion for a second. For he finds fault with them when he says: "The days will come, says the Lord, when I will establish a new covenant with the house of Israel and with the house of

Judah; not like the covenant that I made with their fathers on the day when I took them by the hand to lead them out of the land of Egypt; for they did not continue in my covenant, and so I paid no heed to them, says the Lord."
(Heb. 8:6-9).

The Law of Moses was the first covenant, the Ten Commandments. Now there was nothing wrong with the Ten Commandments and there is still nothing wrong with them. The fault was with the people. God did not find fault with the Law, but verse 8 says, . . . *He finds fault with them,* with the people, for they misunderstood the purpose of the Law, as men and women all over the world today misunderstand the purpose of the Ten Commandments.

The people of that day thought God wanted them to keep these Ten Commandments as the only way they could please Him. They felt He demanded a rigid, careful, scrupulous observance of the Ten Commandments. But what they did not understand, though God pointed this out to them many times, was that God never expected them to keep it. He knew they could not. He did not give it to them to be kept, for He knew they could not keep it. He gave it to them to show them they could not keep it, so they would then be ready to receive a Saviour. But with presumptuous confidence they tried to keep it and when they could not, as of course God knew they could not, they pretended to keep it, just as we do today. We set up a standard for ourselves, or accept the standard of others around us, and we honestly try to keep it; but we cannot, for fallen man simply cannot keep moral law. But rather than admit it, we begin to cover up. We lower the requirements, or excuse our failure by saying, "Well, everybody does it." Or perhaps we argue that it is the intent to keep it that ought to be accepted, or we promise to try harder, and so on the excuses go. This is what happened with Israel.

They pretended to keep the Law and deceived themselves and so they sank lower and lower in the moral strata. At the moment of lowest ebb, when they had so sunk into the darkness of pagan ignorance around them that they were worshiping the filthy abominations of the heathen and were ready to be carried captive into Babylon, God sent the prophet Jeremiah to them. Through Jeremiah He informed them of a permanent program that was yet to come. This program had always been available to them by faith but, one day, God said, it would be made evident to the nation. It is that program we look at now.

This is the covenant that I will make with the house of Israel after those days, says the Lord: I will put my laws into their minds, and write them on their hearts, and I will be their God, and they shall be my people. And they shall not teach every one his fellow or every one his brother, saying, "Know the Lord," for all shall know me, from the least of them to the greatest. For I will be merciful toward their iniquities, and I will remember their sins no more. In speaking of a new covenant he treats the first as obsolete. And what is becoming obsolete and growing old is ready to vanish away.

(Heb. 8:10-13).

When Christians gather about the Table of the Lord, the leader takes the bread and breaks it and distributes it. Then follows the cup. Using the words Jesus used as He instituted this supper, the leader says, *This cup is the new covenant in my blood* (1 Cor. 11:25). Jesus speaks of this as the new arrangement, the new agreement, the new constitution, from which the life of all who know Him will be lived. This is what we mean when we repeat those pregnant words.

This is a covenant or agreement made between the Father and the Son. It is not made between us and God, nor between Israel and God; it is wholly between the Father and the Son. But if any man be "in Christ," everything in this covenant is available to him. Some day Israel, as a nation, will be "in Christ." When they are, these words will be fulfilled for Israel, as Jeremiah predicted. But right now, for Jew and Gentile alike, for any individual on the face of the earth who is willing to be "in Christ," to let Christ live in him, this agreement is valid.

Notice there are four provisions of the new constitution. God says, *I will put my laws into their minds, and write them on their hearts.* Right there is the answer to the problem of human motivation. Have you discovered that the problem in your life is not uncertainty as to what is right; you have known that a long time. The problem is you don't want to do it! It is a problem of motivation. Someone has well said, "Our difficulty today is not that we are overstrained; we are simply under-motivated." So the new arrangement, this new constitution, makes provision for that. We are to look to Christ when we are confronted with the thing we do not want to do. When we need a shove, an impetus, we are to say, "Lord Jesus, You have promised to write Your laws in my mind and on my heart, that I may will to do what You want me to do." Then for His dear sake, we do it. Those who have tried it have discovered this works! There is a new motive, a motor (these come from the same word), a new power to do what ought to be done.

Then He says, *I will be their God, and they shall be my people.* What an answer to the search for identification, to the hunger to belong to someone. Here is the answer to the aching question of the human heart: Who am I, anyway? What can I identify with? God says, "You will be identified with me, forever. I will be your God, and you will be my people."

Then there is the promise, *They shall not teach every one his fellow or every one his brother, saying, "Know the Lord," for all shall know me, from the least of them to the greatest.* Here is the answer to the sigh of humanity for a hero. There is in the human heart a desperate hunger for a hero. We want to look up to someone, we want to know some great one personally. God says, "I will satisfy that in your life. You shall know Me!" Do you know the one thing that one true Christian can never say to another Christian, anywhere in the world, is, "Know the Lord." For this is the one thing that is always true of even the youngest Christian, he knows the Lord. That is where we start in Christian living. It is the least common denominator.

Then the last thing, *For I will be merciful toward*

their iniquities, and I will remember their sins no more. This is the answer to the universal sense of condemnation. At a men's conference one of the men said, "You know, I have a most difficult boss. I never know where I stand with him." Do we not often feel that way about God? We say, "I never know where I stand with God." But God says if you are looking to the great High Priest who is ministering to you all the effects of His sacrifice, this is never a problem. For He has written it down in no uncertain words: *There is therefore now no condemnation to them which are in Christ Jesus*[1] (Rom. 8:1). None! He says He is always *for* you, He is never against you. It does not mean He ignores iniquity, but He says, "I will be merciful toward it." When you acknowledge it there is no reproach–and no rehash! He never gets historical, dredging up the past. God never does this!

Now all of this is continuously available. That is the joy of it–always available from within, ministered to us constantly, if we will have it. Someone said at the close of the conference that he was going back home to help a group that needed a shot in the arm. I understood what he meant, but I must confess, I am awfully weary of shots in the arm!

What a hideous figure that is of Christian inspiration! Are we some kind of religious dope addicts with nothing to show for thirty years of Christian life but an armful of needle marks? I much prefer the scriptural figure, *rivers of living water,* from which I can drink and in which I can bathe any time I need it. Listen to the way Horatius Bonar puts it,

"I heard the voice of Jesus say,

'Behold, I freely give
The living water; thirsty one,
Stoop down and drink, and live.'
I came to Jesus, and I drank
Of that life-giving stream;
My thirst was quenched, my soul revived,
And now I live in Him."

"Our Father, thank you for this look at the ministry of our great High Priest, a ministry that so many times we have simply ignored, never taken at face value, never taken seriously, but rather looked about in all the broken cisterns of earth to try to find something as a substitute. God forgive us, and help us to claim our heritage in Him, this new agreement for living.
We pray in His name,
Amen."

8

a clear conscience

The ninth chapter of Hebrews may seem to many to be involved and even confusing, but it was perfectly clear to the Hebrew readers to whom this letter was first written. It describes in rather close detail the Tabernacle in the wilderness with its sacrifices and regulations of food, drink and clothing, and therefore seems difficult to us and even a little dull. But it will help greatly to see what the author is driving at. If we start there we shall have everything in perspective. That point is made clear in verses 13 and 14.

For if the sprinkling of defiled persons with the blood of goats and bulls and with the ashes of a heifer sanctifies for the purification of the flesh [in the Tabernacle of old], *how much more shall the blood of Christ, who through the eternal Spirit offered himself without blemish to God, purify your conscience from dead works to serve the living God.*
(Heb. 9:13,14).

The practical effect of Christ's ministry to us is given in these words, *to purify your conscience from dead works.* The problem, then, that is faced in this passage is how to handle a nagging conscience.

We each have a conscience. We may not be able to analyze it and we certainly cannot control it, but we know we all possess one. Conscience has been defined as "That still, small voice that makes you feel smaller still," or, as one little boy put it, "It is that which feels bad when everything else feels good." Conscience is that internal voice that sits in judgment over our will. There is a very common myth abroad that says that conscience is the means by which we tell what is right and what is wrong. But conscience is never that. It is training that tells us what is right or wrong. But when we know what is right or wrong, it is our conscience that insists that we do what we think is right and avoid what we think is wrong. That distinction is very important and needs to be made clear.

Conscience can be very mistaken; it is not a safe guide by itself. It accuses us when we violate whatever moral standard we may have, but that moral standard may be quite wrong when viewed in the light of God's revelation. But conscience also gives approval whenever we fulfill whatever standard we have, though that standard is right or wrong. And conscience, we have all discovered, acts both before and after the fact–it can either prod or punish.

In the case of these Hebrews the problem is not over wrongdoing, it is not a conscience troubled over evil deeds, but "dead works." We must remember that the readers of this letter are Christians who already know how to handle the problem of sins. When they become aware that they have deliberately disobeyed what they knew to be right, they know the only way they can quiet an avenging conscience is to confess the sin before God, and deal with the problem immediately. That aspect of a troubled conscience can easily be taken care of by Christians as they accept the forgiving grace of God. But the problem here is a conscience plagued with guilt over good left undone. Not sins of commission, but sins of omission.

These people try to put their conscience to rest by religious activity; they are goaded by an uneasy conscience into a high-gear program in order to please God. Here are people who are intent on doing what is right and thus pleasing God; they have therefore launched upon an intensive program of religious activity which may range all the way from bead-counting and candle-burning to serving on committees, passing out tracts, teaching Sunday School classes, or what-have-you. What perceptible difference in motive is there between a poor, blinded pagan who, in his misconception of truth, crawls endlessly down a road to placate God, and an American Christian who busies himself in a continual round of activity to try to win a sense of acceptance before God? None whatsoever! A woman said to me, "I don't know what is the matter with me. I do all I can to serve the Lord but I still feel guilty, and then I feel guilty about feeling guilty!" Precisely! It *is* rather discouraging, is it not, to see that all this laudable effort on our part is dismissed here as *dead works.* It is disconcerting to see that such effort is not acceptably serving God. God is not impressed by our feverish effort.

Well, what do you do when this is your problem? Certainly not try harder; that is the worst thing you could do. Perhaps now we are ready to listen to what the writer says about **the poverty of activity.** Let us start at the first of the chapter. The problem, he points out, is not the nature of what we do; it is not activity itself, for there was, in the Old Testament, a God-authorized place of activity.

Now even the first covenant had regulations for worship and an earthly sanctuary. For a tent was prepared, the outer one, in which were the lampstand and the table and the bread of the Presence; it is called the Holy Place. Behind the second curtain stood a tent called the Holy of Holies, having the golden altar of incense and the ark of the covenant covered on all sides with gold, which contained a golden urn holding the manna, and Aaron's rod that budded, and the tables of the covenant; above it were the cherubim of glory overshadowing the mercy seat. Of these things we cannot now speak in detail.
(Heb. 9:1-5).

And neither can we! The point he makes is, there was nothing wrong with the activity of worship in the Tabernacle. It was God-authorized and perfectly proper. Also, there were God-authorized regulations.

These preparations having thus been made, the priests go continually into the outer tent, performing their ritual duties; but into the second only the high priest

goes, and he but once a year, and not without taking blood which he offers for himself and for the errors of the people. By this the Holy Spirit indicates that the way into the sanctuary is not yet opened as long as the outer tent is still standing (which is symbolic for the present age). According to this arrangement, gifts and sacrifices are offered which cannot perfect the conscience of the worshiper, but deal only with food and drink and various ablutions, regulations for the body imposed until the time of reformation.
(Heb. 9:6-10).

All of these activities had to do with the Old Testament, the worship in the Tabernacle, and the regulations connected with it. But the writer is simply pointing out there were three drastic limitations to these.

First, if these Old Testament worshipers saw no deeper than the ordinance they were performing, the only benefit would be to the body. The writer says, *According to this arrangement, gifts and sacrifices are offered which cannot perfect the conscience . . . but deal only with food and drink and various ablutions, regulations for the body.* Because these affected only the outer man, there was no change in the inner man. The performance of a service, a ritual, a sacrifice, or an ordinance, does not do anything to the performer, it only affects the part of the body involved in the performance.

In baptism the whole body is cleansed; if it is kneeling or bowing then only the part of the body involved is affected. This is his argument: no ritual or ordinance has value in itself. This needs to be declared again and again in the hearing of men. We are so convinced that God places value in ordinances. No, the writer says that even in this God-authorized system there was no value in what was done. He makes that very clear. The conscience was not touched and therefore gave the worshiper no rest, continually hounding him, making him feel guilty, dragging him back to perform the same thing over and over again in a restless search for peace. It was like a man who goes down and buys a new suit every time he needs a bath. His solution never touches the real problem, but keeps covering it over. Eventually that kind of a person becomes very difficult to live with, as are also those who place value on ordinances.

The second point he makes is, these ordinances were intended to have a deeper message. They are symbolic, he says, for the present age. No ritual had meaning in itself, it had meaning in what it stood for. That is the point. It was intended to convey a deeper message. The Tabernacle worship, with all these strange provisions–the bread, the incense, the offerings, the ornate building itself with its altars–all was a kind of religious play enacted to teach the people what was going on in their inner life. They were not to place importance upon the outward drama–that was only a play–it was what it stood for that was important. But they completely missed the point and thought God was interested in the ritual. In chapter 10 the author of Hebrews will quote Christ as saying very plainly, *in burnt offerings and sin offerings thou hast taken no pleasure* (v. 6). God was never interested in ritual. It meant nothing to Him.

The third point he makes is that these things will

never touch the conscience, reach the inner man, or do anything effective until men accept this fact that religious activity, or ritual, is only a picture and has no value in itself at all. As he says, *The Holy Spirit indicates that the way into the sanctuary* [the real inner man] *is not yet opened as long as the outer tent* [the Tabernacle] *is still standing.* "Is still standing" is a mistranslation. It should be "still has any standing," or "still has any value in their sight." In other words, they could never see what God was driving at as long as they had their attention focused on the ritual. They could never realize the value intended until they saw behind the ritual to what God was saying. Until they saw the total worthlessness of outward things to do anything for them, they could never begin to appropriate the real message.

There are some in the Old Testament who did see this. You cannot read David's experience recorded in the Fifty-first Psalm without seeing that he understood this. That psalm was written after the terrible twin failure of adultery and murder into which he fell. And he was the king! In the psalm he confesses that God brought conviction to his heart, yet he says, *For thou desirest not sacrifice; else would I give it: thou delightest not in burnt offering. The sacrifices of God are a broken spirit: a broken and contrite heart, O God, thou wilt not despise*[1] (Ps. 51:16,17).

David understood the worthlessness of mere ritual. That is why he is called "a man after God's own heart." But the rest of the people, by and large, missed the point. So they were goaded by their conscience into an endless routine of religious activity, until they came near despair.

In contrast to this the writer sets before us *the power of reality.*

But when Christ appeared as a high priest of the good things that have come, then through the greater and more perfect tent (not made with hands, that is, not of this creation) he entered once for all into the Holy Place, taking not the blood of goats and calves but his own blood, thus securing an eternal redemption. For if the sprinkling of defiled persons with the blood of goats and bulls and with the ashes of a heifer sanctifies for the purification of the flesh, how much more shall the blood of Christ, who through the eternal Spirit offered himself without blemish to God, purify your conscience from dead works to serve the living God. (Heb. 9:11-14).

Do you see the argument? He is saying the first arrangement, depending upon the activity of the worshiper (that is the point) affected only the body.

If you are trying to do something for God, if you are involved in activity on His behalf, all it ever affects is the outer man, the body. It never quiets the conscience. It cannot, for it does not get below the surface: it does not touch that area. But the second arrangement, the new constitution by which Christians are to live, depends not on the work of the worshiper but on the activity of Christ in our place! Therefore it moves through the barrier of the flesh into the Holy of Holies, the inner spirit, the inner man. When the conscience, in there, is confronted with the value of Christ's blood, it has nothing to say! Do you see the point?

He is declaring that our activity adds nothing to our acceptance before God. God does not like us better because we serve Him. Oh, to get this point across! Our service, our faithful works on His behalf, our labors, our diligent efforts to do something for God, never make Him think one bit better or worse of us. God does not love you because you serve Him; God loves you because He is love! He accepts you because you believe in Christ. That is the only reason. Therefore, serving is no more a duty, and if we see it in that light it becomes delight.

An article in the *Sunday School Times,* titled "The Great Saboteur," details the work of Satan as the great accuser of the brethren. He is the one who stimulates the conscience to nag, drive, goad and prod us, and to keep us feeling a vague sense of hazy, undefined guilt before God. That is the work of the accuser, the saboteur. Here are some revealing sentences.

Scripture recognizes, as the Accuser also does, that nothing so impedes your access to God as a guilty conscience. You can't draw near boldly unless your heart is *sprinkled clean from an evil conscience* (Heb. 10:22). Therefore, if you want to overcome Satan at this point, don't just talk to him about the blood of Christ.

Instead, accept the fact that the blood of Christ completely satisfies God about you. Remind yourself that God welcomes you into His presence not on the grounds of your Christian progress, the depth of your knowledge, or even the degree of victory you have found, but on the grounds of the blood of the Lamb.

The discovery of this glorious secret has enabled

saints down the ages to overcome the Accuser, *they overcame him by the blood of the Lamb.* They did not remind him of the blood of Christ, they reminded themselves. They refused to wilt before his accusations and were, therefore, able to enjoy free access to the throne of grace and full liberty in their service.

That is helpful, is it not? These overcomers did not keep looking always at their inner condition, they looked rather to the solution that God had given to the problem.

Right at this point any thoughtful person will raise a question which frequently nags Christians and is often voiced by the enemies of Christian faith. Someone may well ask, "Why does this have to be by blood? Why is a death necessary?" The Christian gospel rests upon the blood sacrifice of Jesus Christ, and this fact has been a source of much criticism and a stumbling block to many people. Christianity has been sneeringly referred to as "the religion of the slaughterhouse" and the gospel has been called "the gospel of gore" because of this continual emphasis upon the need for blood, for death. It is this mark of finality which the writer now examines.

Therefore he is the mediator of a new covenant, so that those who are called may receive the promised eternal inheritance, since a death has occurred which redeems them from the transgressions under the first covenant. For where a will is involved, the death of the one who made it must be established. For a will takes effect only at death, since it is not in force as long as the one who made it is alive. Hence even the first covenant was not ratified without blood. For when every commandment of the law had been declared by Moses to all the people, he took the blood of calves and goats, with water and scarlet wool and hyssop, and sprinkled both the book itself and all the people, saying, "This is the blood of the covenant which God commanded you." And in the same way he sprinkled with the blood both the tent and all the vessels used in worship. Indeed, under the law almost everything is purified with blood, and without the shedding of blood there is no forgiveness of sins.

Thus it was necessary for the copies of the heavenly things to be purified with these rites, but the heavenly things themselves with better sacrifices than these. (Heb. 9:15-23).

Without a death, he argues, it is not possible to receive the benefits of the covenant God makes. For, he points out, no will that is written can bestow any benefits until after the death of the maker. I met with a group of men and women to whom the director of a Christian Conference Center was explaining certain of the procedures involved in securing additional property for the expansion of the ministry. He described one case where a deed had been executed by the owner of the property, a widow. He explained that she was to be paid an annuity until her death, and on her death the property would become the property of the Conference Association. Someone immediately raised his hand and facetiously asked, "How healthy is she?" The question was not in good taste but it illustrates the point. Wills are of no value to the beneficiaries until the death of the testator, the will maker. This is what the writer here argues.

You cannot avail yourself of all that Jesus Christ provides for you in terms of release from a guilty conscience, unless there is a death. The will is useless without it. In fact, he says, death is so important that even the shadow, the picture in the Old Testament, required blood. Not, of course, the blood of Jesus Christ, but the blood of bulls and goats. Blood is inescapable. Now that brings us to the point. Why? We shall never come to the answer till we squarely face the implications of the substitutionary character of the death of Jesus Christ. His death was not for His own sake, it was for ours. He was our representative. It was not so much His blood that was shed, but ours. This is what God is so desperately trying to convey to us.

The cross is God's way of saying there is nothing in us worth saving at all, apart from Christ—no salvageable content whatsoever. He takes us as we are, men and women apart from Christ, and He says, "There is nothing you can do for Me, not one thing." For when Christ became what we are, when He was "made sin for us," God passed sentence upon Him, and put Him to death. This is God's eloquent way of saying to us, "There is nothing to please Me, in yourself. There is not a thing you can do by your own effort that is worth a thing." All that we can ever be, without Christ, is totally set aside. Death eliminates us, wipes us out.

That is why our activity does not improve our relationship with Him in the least degree. It does not make us any more acceptable, even though it is activity for Him. See what this does to our human pride. It cuts the ground right out from under us.

Who has not heard Christians talking in such a way as to give the impression that the greatest thing that ever happened to God was the day He found them. But we are not indispensable to Him; He is indispensable to us. And the great truth to which this brings us is, if we become unable to do anything for God, we are then able to receive everything from Him. That is what He wants us to see.

That is why verse 14 closes with this wonderful news that the blood of Christ purifies our conscience to serve the living God. The gospel is that He has made Himself available to us, to do everything in us, as a living God. *Faithful is he that calleth you, who also will do it*[1] (1 Thess. 5:24). The one who calls you to do something is the one who intends to do it, through you. Therefore, let us stop thinking we have to depend on our intellect, our ability, our gifts, our talents, or our anything and start reckoning on His ability to supply what we need to do what He asks. He can say with Paul, *I can do all things through Christ which strengtheneth me*[1] (Phil. 4:13). Do you understand that? What a relief that is!

But the point of the whole passage is, if we refuse to reckon this way, to count this to be true, if we refuse this, then there are no benefits of the new covenant available to us. A covenant is not in effect until there is the death of the testator, the death of the will maker. It is we, through Christ our representative, who died that death. But if we will not accept it, if we will not agree to this and accept God's sentence of death upon all that we are, then we cannot have the benefits. That is what he is saying. If we fight this sentence of death, for the rest of our Christian lives we shall be troubled with a guilty conscience. We will never rest in any final acceptance before God. We shall always be wrestling with the problem of whether we have done enough and have been pleasing to God by our activity. But if we accept this, the effect is to render service pure delight.

A mission leader and I were discussing a young man whose very obvious, evident, earnest desire is to be used of God. This young man desperately hopes to be used, he wants to be in a place of leadership, he wants to exercise power in his ministry. But every time he is given the opportunity to try, somehow something about the way he does it, the attitude he displays in it, immediately begins to create personality problems. Every effort he makes along this line comes to nothing. Eventually, he himself is overwhelmed with a sense of frustration and utter defeat. He experiences this over and over simply because he will not accept the fact that is proclaimed here in Hebrews: that God has ruled him out, that there are no talents he has that he can employ in any service, any worthwhile, acceptable service to God. As long as he is still struggling to use his abilities to do something for God it will never be acceptable—and neither will yours, nor mine!

By contrast, I listened to another young man and his wife tell about how God had brought them through various struggles and trials until they had come to the place where, as he said, "Three months ago God broke through and I learned something that I have known all my life but I didn't understand up till this point. I have learned what is the meaning of that verse, *If any man will come after me, let him deny himself*[1] (Luke 9:23). I always thought that meant self-denial, that meant giving up certain things or places or position for Christ, but I never learned until now that means I must deny my self, that I have no right to my self, that I have no abilities in my self, but that I can have everything in Christ. My life from that moment on has been a totally different thing." His wife, sitting by his side, kept nodding her head and smiling, which is the greatest testimony of all that this works. Look on to the end of the book, in chapter 13, that well-known benediction we quote so frequently,

Now may the God of peace who brought again from the dead our Lord Jesus, the great shepherd of the sheep, by the blood of the eternal covenant, equip you with everything good that you may do his will, working in you [there is the secret] *that which is pleasing in his sight* (vv. 20,21). That is the secret of a clear conscience.

"Our Father, open our eyes to this new principle of human behavior. Teach us to grasp this, Lord, and to accept Your sentence of death upon everything in us that is not of Christ, and to recognize that in Him, by Him, through Him we can do everything that needs to be done by us. Through Him who loves us and who strengthens us.
In His name,
Amen."

9

the unfolding pattern

Hebrews is the book that distinguishes clearly between the shell of Christianity and the real meat of it. It helps us to see the difference between shadow and substance, the picture and reality. A man would be a fool who would prefer reading a cookbook to eating a good meal when he is hungry. Not that there is anything wrong with reading a cookbook—it can be very enlightening—but it is not very nourishing. Yet many a Christian concerns himself with the externals of Christian faith and misses completely the dynamic, radical, revolutionary concepts of it. Jesus did not say, "You should know the rules and be bound by them." What He said was, *You will know the truth, and the truth will make you free* (John 8:32). That is such a different thing!

Now the author of Hebrews tells us that Christianity is not a mere set of rules. Christianity is not something you do for your country, your city, your home, yourself, or your God. Christianity is what God does in you and for you. Hebrews contrasts the new arrangement for living with the old basis of trying to keep the rules. We lean very strongly toward rule-keeping.

Someone has likened humanity to a man who fell down a well. When he cried out for help a passerby, hearing his cries, leaned over the well and asked him what he wanted. The man said he wanted to get out. The fellow thought for a moment and finally took out a piece of paper and wrote something on it and dropped it down into the well. When the man picked it up he read, "Ten Rules on How to Keep Out of Wells." It has been suggested that this is what the law has been to us; a set of rules on how to keep out of wells after we have fallen in. In many ways this is accurate. But the real problem is that man does not know that he has fallen down a well. He thinks he was made to live in wells, and therefore he cannot understand why he is so unhappy in the well. The coming of the Law, the Ten Commandments, has made him realize his plight but it still cannot help him out. This is what the author of Hebrews is telling us. He is saying that Jesus Christ is a rope dropped into the well; and more than that, He is a winch to pull man out, and a guide to keep him from falling in any more wells after he gets out.

In some wonderful way, the Tabernacle in the wilderness, with its regulations and sacrifices, was a marvelous picture of the work of Jesus Christ and the new arrangement for living which would be available to men in Christ. But only up to a point. It was both a comparison and a contrast, both like it and unlike it, as any picture must be. I carry a picture of my wife in my wallet and when I am away from home I find it comforting to look at it, but it is very inadequate, it is not my wife. I can look at the picture but I cannot have a conversation with it, I cannot laugh together with it, I cannot kiss it or, if I did, it would not be very satisfying, and I cannot persuade it to cook any meals. Though it is an accurate representation of the real thing, it is a far cry from it. That is what Hebrews stresses. In the section before us the author concludes his explanation of the new arrangement for living in Jesus Christ, by listing for us the advantages in contrast to the picture of the Tabernacle.

For Christ has entered, not into a sanctuary made with hands, a copy of the true one, but into heaven itself, now to appear in the presence of God on our behalf. Nor was it to offer himself repeatedly, as the high priest enters the Holy Place yearly with blood not his own; for then he would have had to suffer repeatedly since the foundation of the world. But as it is, he has appeared once for all at the end of the age to put away sin by the sacrifice of himself. And just as it is appointed for men to die once, and after that comes judgment, so Christ, having been offered once to bear the sins of many, will appear a second time, not to deal with sin but to save those who are eagerly waiting for him.
(Heb. 9:24-28).

The old system, with its regulations, rituals and sacrifices, was limited to one particular place, the Tabernacle, including the sanctuary made by hands, the holy of holies. But the writer says in Christ a new arrangement has come in which is **beyond space.** It is not limited to space, it is heaven. We have already suggested that heaven is the realm of the spirit. It is a new dimension of life. It is the inner man. Some have been troubled by this and have wondered if I no longer believe that heaven is a place. Yes, heaven is a place, for spirit can be related to a place. Our spirits dwell in bodies and by such they are limited constantly to place. But the idea of heaven in the Scriptures is not primarily that of place. We distort it when we limit it to place, as in the concept that heaven is off in space somewhere and we die and go to heaven by being transported across the reaches of space. Scripture reveals here that when Jesus Christ makes the spirit alive within, He thus brings heaven into the soul, into the heart. There is an old hymn we sing which catches the idea exactly.

"Since Christ my soul from sin set free
This world has been a heaven to me
And 'mid earth's sorrows and its woes
'Tis heaven my Jesus here to know."

This new dimension of living is heaven here on earth. It is this that makes it possible for the apostle Paul to write to the Ephesians and say, *Ye are now seated with Christ in the heavenlies* (See Eph. 2:6). Heaven is in our heart because Christ is there. It is God who makes heaven, heaven. Heaven is the new dimension of life in the spirit. When I die and "go to heaven" I simply enter into this relationship in a new and greater way than I have experienced in the body. It will certainly involve the concept of place. For since we will have resurrection bodies, there must be some place for them to operate and wherever that place is, is heaven.

If you grasp this concept you will see that the writer is indicating here that Christ's work for me is never hindered because of where I am, for He is within me. Therefore He appears before the presence of God on my behalf within me. That work is going on all the time, unceasingly, unendingly for me, within me, therefore wherever I am it is available to me. This is the point he is making.

"I know not where his islands lift
Their fronded palms in air.
I only know I cannot drift
Beyond his love and care."*

Then, he points out that the old system required endless repetition of sacrifice. The effect of these sacrifices never lasted very long. A man had to bring a fresh sacrifice every time he sinned, and once a year the whole nation had to offer the same sacrifice, year after year. The old arrangement required repetition. But the new arrangement is **beyond time,** as well as beyond space. The cross of Christ is a contemporary sacrifice: it was offered at one point in history, but the effect of it, the results and blessings of it, are available at any time, forward or backward from that point of history. Thus the Old Testament saints could have as much of Christ as we can, for all that He was in His sacrifice was as fully available to them

---

*John Greenleaf Whittier, *The Eternal Goodness,* Stanza 20

by faith as it is by faith to us who live on this side of the cross. This means the cross works as well in this twentieth century as it did in the first century, and that it judges my pride and evil as relentlessly after I have been a Christian for thirty years as it does when I first come to Christ. It is a contemporary event and therefore no penance or remorse on my part can ever add anything to it. It is always effective for it is timeless. What a great advantage this is over the old system!

Then, third, the new arrangement is **beyond judgment** as well as beyond time and space. In the Tabernacle the high priest went into the holy of holies once a year, bearing with him the blood of a lamb. Before he entered, on that day only, he stripped off his garments of beauty and glory and clothed himself in a simple white robe. He took the blood of a lamb in a basin and went into the holy of holies while the people waited with trepidation and fear outside, wondering if the sacrifice would be acceptable before God. If it was not, the whole nation would be wiped out; for when the high priest went in he was facing the judgment of God.

In this eloquent way God was saying to those people that judgment awaits a man when he dies. As the writer points out here, *It is appointed for men to die once, and after that comes judgment.* But when the high priest came out again, he did not appear in his white robe. Before he came again to the people he dressed himself in his robes of beauty and glory once again, and came out to meet with rejoicing and thanksgiving on the part of the people. That was a picture, the writer says, of what is true in the reality that Christ represents. Christ has entered by death into the realm of our spirit, into the human heart, into the inner life of man, and therefore He is now invisible to the world. They do not see Him. But when He appears visibly again it will not be to judge the world—the cross has already done that—but it will be to establish a time of peace and of glory upon the earth, which we call "the Golden Age," the Millennium. But for the Christian, this judgment is already past, and in the spirit he lives already in the age of peace. The judgment that a man must face when he dies has already been faced when we died in Christ. The judgment has been poured out upon him.

I was born on the windswept plains of North Dakota. I remember as a boy sometimes seeing at night the flames of a prairie fire lighting the horizon, sweeping across the grass of those prairies. Such prairie fires were terrible threats to the pioneers who crossed the plains in their covered wagons. Often these fires would burn for miles and miles, threatening everything in their path. When they would see such a fire coming toward them, driven before the wind, they had a device they would use to protect themselves. They would simply light another fire and the wind would catch it up and drive it on beyond them and then they would get in the burned-over place and when the fire coming toward them reached it, it found nothing to burn and went out. God is saying that the cross of Jesus Christ is such a burned-over place. Those who trust in it, and rest in the judgment that has already been visited upon it, have no other judgment to face. That is why Paul can write with such triumph in Romans 8, *There is therefore now no condemnation for those who are in Christ Jesus* (v. 1). In the realm of the spirit we have already entered into triumph and glory, we have already been forgiven everything. We need now only to acknowledge wrong, confess it, and the moment we do forgiveness is already ours. We need only to say thank you for it and take it.

Have you found this? What a release from the nagging pressure and distress that is caused by a guilty conscience.

Now the question comes, "Has this kind of life been demonstrated?" The next section sets before us the demonstration of this new arrangement in Christ. It can be seen both in shadowy outline in the Tabernacle, and in the reality of Jesus Christ Himself. In the Tabernacle you see *the divine design.*

For since the law has but a shadow of the good things to come instead of the true form of these realities, it can never, by the same sacrifices which are continually offered year after year, make perfect those who draw near. Otherwise, would they not have ceased to be offered? If the worshipers had once been cleansed, they would no longer have any consciousness of sin. But in these sacrifices there is a reminder of sin year after year. For it is impossible that the blood of bulls and goats should take away sins.
(Heb. 10:1-4).

There is limitation evident all through this. There is much these things could not portray because they are not reality, they are merely pictures, shadows of reality. The blood of bulls and goats is not the blood of Christ, therefore it cannot take away sin. But through this limitation there is one unchanging message being pounded out. Every sacrifice of old declared it; every offering told the same story; it was burned in blood and smoke into every listening heart. That message was that the essential quality in a God-approved life is that one be willing to lay that life down. Every sacrifice was a life laid down. By it God is saying that this is the quality of life that pleases Him; a life laid down, self-giving, not self-loving.

There is a twisted form of Christianity abroad today that says in effect, "I believe that Jesus died on the cross in order that I might be free to live for myself; that He bore all the pain and suffering, therefore there is nothing like that for me to bear at all. If I am asked to endure pain or difficulty or heartache, something is wrong because Christ bore all that for me." That is a distorted form of Christian faith. The truth is that Jesus died in order that I might be free to die with Him, and He rose again in order that I might be privileged to rise with Him. This is a timeless thing; it goes on all the time. We must forever be doing this. You will never know the rising without the dying: that is the secret of Christian faith. Unless we are willing to lay down our lives we can never have them back again. Is that not what Jesus said? *Whosoever will save his life shall lose it: and whosoever will lose his life for my sake shall find it*[1] (Matt. 16:25). We can never save our life until we are willing to lay it down.

But the wonderful thing is, if we are continually

dying with Him, we shall also be continually rising with Him. If in our hearts there is a readiness to give ourselves on His behalf in the service of others, we shall find in that dying that we are also rising, living again. Life takes on new dimension. That is the great secret. The Old Testament sacrifices taught that there had to be a death, but that was the teaching of the shadow. Now see it in the living substance of the flesh of Christ Himself. The Old Testament revealed the divine design, but in Christ we advance to see *the divine desire.*

Consequently, when Christ came into the world, he said, "Sacrifices and offerings thou hast not desired, but a body hast thou prepared for me; in burnt offerings and sin offerings thou hast taken no pleasure. Then I said, 'Lo, I have come to do thy will, O God,' as it is written of me in the roll of the book." When he said above, "Thou hast neither desired nor taken pleasure in sacrifices and offerings and burnt offerings and sin offerings" (these are offered according to the law), then he added, "Lo, I have come to do thy will." He abolishes the first in order to establish the second. And by that will we have been sanctified through the offering of the body of Jesus Christ once for all.
(Heb. 10:5-10).

Here is what God really wanted. God never cared a snap of His fingers for all the rivers of blood that flowed on Jewish altars.

"Not all the blood of beasts
    on Jewish altars slain,

Could give the guilty conscience rest
or wash away one stain."

He did not delight in these; He had no interest in them except as they taught something. Well then, what was He after? What these sacrifices pointed to: a human body in which there was a human will which continually chose to depend upon an indwelling God to obey a written Word! That was what He was after, that was what God wanted. When Christ came He paused on the threshold of heaven and said, "A body hast thou prepared for me." There in the womb of the virgin a human body was being formed, a body with nerve and muscle and sinew and hair and eyes and feet, growing through all the stages that the normal human embryo goes through. Within that body was a human soul with the capacity to reason, to feel and to choose–a will, in other words.

That will, in that human body, never once acted on its own, never once took any step apart from dependence upon the Father who dwelt within. Jesus declared this over and over again, *The things that I do, I do not do of Myself, but the Father who dwells in Me, He does them. The words that I speak are not My words, it is the Father who is speaking through Me, He is saying them to you* (John 14:10, Author's Translation). There was a will which continually chose to rely upon the Father to guide that life step by step in every experience, and to meet everything that came with the strength of an indwelling life. Now that is the principle that God has been after all along; that is what He wants.

God has no interest in ritual, in candles, in prayer

books, in beads, in chanting, in any ceremony. Ceremonies mean nothing to God. What He wants is a heart that is His, a life that is His, and a body that is available to Him. That is why Paul in Romans 12:1 says, *I beseech you therefore, brethren, by the mercies of God, that ye present your bodies a living sacrifice, holy, acceptable unto God, which is your reasonable service* [that is, your expected task, what you were designed to do].[1] When our Lord Jesus acted on that principle He allowed the direction of His life to come from the Word of God. *Then I said, "Lo, I have come to do thy will, O God," as it is written of me in the roll of the book* (Heb. 10:7).

Every temptation He entered into, every problem that came His way, He referred back to what God had said: "It is written," "It is written," "It is written. . . ." That program took Him to the cross, calling on Him to lay down His life. And by means of that sacrifice, we are free now to join Him on this program that is God's original intention for man. You see this in verse 10. *And by that will we* [believers] *have been sanctified through the offering of the body of Jesus Christ once for all.*

This word "sanctified" is widely misunderstood. It is usually looked upon as some kind of religious sheep-dip that people pass through and they come out holier and purer on the other side. But it is not that. The word "sanctified" simply means, "to put to the proper, intended use." You sanctify a chair when you sit in it. You sanctify your comb when you comb your hair. Sanctification simply means to put to the intended purpose. Now this verse is simply declaring that when we adopt the same outlook as

Jesus Christ–when, in dependence on Him, we are ready to obey the Word of God and thus fulfill the will of God, we fulfill our humanity. We are being used in the way God intended us to be used.

There is one simple mark of that which is unmistakable: we become content to lay down our lives in order that the will of God be done! I do not mean we rush out to die. Laying down a life does not always mean dying, it means giving of yourself, giving up for the moment something that you might desire to do. It means that we become content to lose standing, if necessary, in the eyes of the world. We no longer regard that as important in our lives. It means we give up material comfort or gain if this will advance the cause of Christ. We live in a simpler home in order that we might invest money in His enterprises. We are willing to be ignored, or slighted, or treated unfairly if, in the doing of it, God's cause will get ahead. We are willing to feel inadequate in ourselves in order that we might always be adequate in Him. Do you see what I am talking about?

That sounds hard and demanding, perhaps, but it is not. It is joyful, it is glorious. His yoke is easy and His burden is light. We got involved in a week of witnessing in Newport Beach, California. Ten men went down at their own expense, some of them taking their vacations, using time that they would otherwise like to have for themselves. They worked from six o'clock in the morning till midnight all through the week, in the most demanding type of work, exposing themselves in situations that often could have been highly embarrassing. And why? Because they were yielding their bodies to God to advance His work.

Without exception, every one of those men said that this was one of the greatest weeks of his life, a most thrilling time. They learned one thing above all else; that this business of being available to God to use in any situation is what we used to call in the Navy "S.O.P."–Standard Operating Procedure! There is nothing new about it, nothing unusual; it is the standard thing. This is what God wants, this is what He is after. Not great cathedrals and beautiful buildings and ornate ritual and ceremony: God does not care for those. God wants lives, bodies, hearts that are His, available to Him to work in the shop and the office and the street and the schools and everywhere man is, that His life may be made visible in terms of that person, in that place. That is Christianity.

Now notice in the closing section, the new arrangement and *its sufficiency.*

And every priest stands daily at his service, offering repeatedly the same sacrifices, which can never take away sins. But when Christ has offered for all time a single sacrifice for sins, he sat down at the right hand of God, then to wait until his enemies should be made a stool for his feet. For by a single offering he has perfected for all time those who are sanctified. And the Holy Spirit also bears witness to us; for after saying, "This is the covenant that I will make with them after those days, says the Lord: I will put my laws on their hearts, and write them on their minds," then he adds, "I will remember their sins and their misdeeds no more." Where there is forgiveness of these, there is no longer any offering for sin.
(Heb. 10:11-18).

One peculiarity of the old Tabernacle was that it had no chairs. There was never a place for the priests to sit down, for they had continually to be ministering. But when Christ offered Himself as a single sacrifice He sat down, the writer says, to wait until His enemies should be made His footstool. Why? Because the principle that He demonstrated is, that is all that it takes to get the job done. It does not need anything more; He has done all that is needed. Once this principle has begun in human history it will never stop until it wins what God is after, until all the enemies of Christ become His footstool and it is time to return again to establish His kingdom.

There is a power in this principle that is quiet and yet obstinate, relentless, irresistible. Where men and women are willing to lay down their lives, nothing can hinder them, nothing can arrest this principle, nothing can stop it. It is bound to win. One of the men who went with us to witness in Newport Beach was a prominent scientist-engineer. One day at a breakfast he stood up before some fifty or sixty men to speak to them about his faith in Christ, and he told in rather dramatic detail of the feeling he had when he pushed the plunger that detonated the first hydrogen bomb at Bikini Atoll. He knew he would release the awesome power of a bomb that would literally obliterate the island upon which the test occurred, and no man really knew for sure what else would happen. But he said, "I want you men to know that I am more scared right now than I was then." There was, of course, the fear of standing before a group of strangers to talk to them about faith, but he was also aware that he was now releasing a power that was far greater than the H-bomb. Through the channel of his life and testimony he was being used as an instrument of God to release a power that would not destroy, blast and ruin, but was the only power that man has ever known that restores and brings together, heals and makes life whole.

That is why Jesus sat down. What else was there to do? It is all finished, it is sufficient, it is adequate. It will win the prize, it will do the job. When you have rested upon all Jesus Christ has done for you, you have entered into a place of provision of power. *I will put my laws into their minds, and write them on their hearts* (Heb. 8:10). You can know in any situation what God wants done and expect Him to do it through you. More than that, you enter into perfect peace of heart. There is no quarrel between you and God any longer; you are accepted in the Beloved. *I will remember their sins no more* (Heb. 8:12). Now, the writer says, when you come to this place, what more do you need? Where there is forgiveness, there is no more offering for sins needed. Of course not. Man has drawn near to God, the relationship is complete.

"Our Father, though it may take us many years of struggle and effort to learn this principle of ceasing from our own efforts and resting quietly upon Your ability to work in us, nevertheless, Lord, when we learn it, what release, what relief there is, what a joy to stop our straining, fretful, petulant efforts to please You and do something for You, and simply to rest upon Your willingness to do everything in and through us. What grace, Lord, to make this known to us. We pray that we may learn to rest upon this new arrangement and thus be equipped to enter into every situation, face any circumstance or any problem with the adequacy which is Yours, available to us. In Christ's name,
Amen."

10

triumph or tragedy

Most of the arguments that are launched against the Christian faith today are based on a caricature of Christianity, a distorted view. When the world once sees the real thing it has little to say in opposition. It is this true faith which the book of Hebrews so masterfully sets forth before us. It reveals clearly the difference between the false and the true. The false way of living as a Christian is to believe and try harder. That is the Avis Car Rental motto "We Try Harder," and it appears in the common attitude, "I'll do my best and God will do the rest." Now that sounds deceptively pious, even sanctimonious and very Christian, but it is utterly false! As we have been seeing in Hebrews, the true way is to believe and fully trust, for God is in you, both to will and to work His good pleasure. Your willing is therefore His willing, unless He shows you differently; your working is His working, unless He shows you otherwise.

The last half of chapter 10 sums it all up for us. The writer of this letter is drawing his presentation of the teaching of this passage to a conclusion. He strikes again the three dominant notes of the letter—teaching, warning and encouragement. More precisely, verses 19 through 39 reveal a provision which creates privilege, a presumption which invites punishment, and a fortitude which reveals faith. That is our guide to understanding.

In a nutshell, the secret of Christian living is described in this first section, **the provision which creates privilege.**

Therefore, brethren, since we have confidence to enter the sanctuary by the blood of Jesus, by the new and living way which he opened for us through the curtain, that is, through his flesh, and since we have a great high priest over the house of God, let us draw near with a true heart in full assurance of faith, with our hearts sprinkled clean from an evil conscience and our bodies washed with pure water. Let us hold fast the confession of our hope without wavering, for he who promised is faithful; and let us consider how to stir up one another to love and good works, not neglecting to meet together, as is the habit of some, but encouraging one another, and all the more as you see the Day drawing near.
(Heb. 10:19-25).

Looking carefully at that passage you note twice the phrase, *we have.* And following these there is repeated three times the phrase, *let us. We have* marks provision; *let us* is privilege.

What do we have? *We have confidence,* he says, *we have boldness to enter into the sanctuary.* That is not a church building! I have a continuing quarrel against the practice of calling church buildings "sanctuaries." I understand what people mean by this, but I regard it as a very insidious concept, for, as I have pointed out before, there is no building on the face of the earth today that is properly called the house of God. If we call a building the house of God we miss the true message of the New Testament, which is that the house of God is actually the bodies of men and women, boys and girls. That is where God dwells today. The true sanctuary, therefore, is the realm of the spirit in man. It is pictured in the Tabernacle. We have the outer court in the body, the holy place in the soul, and the holy of holies is the spirit of man. It was this into which we were forbidden to enter as long as we did not know Jesus Christ. We could not move into the realm of the spirit. Our spirits, the Bible says, were *dead in trespasses and sins*[1] (Eph. 2:1). But through the blood of Christ a way has been opened into this area. When we became Christians, for the first time we were able to operate on a spiritual level. Our spirits began to function. We became, for the first time, complete human beings, operating as God intended man to operate.

It is this inner man that the writer is referring to as the sanctuary. We now come with boldness, he says, into the inner man, into the realm of the spirit, where we meet face to face with God. The spirit is the only part of man that can meet God. Unfortunately, there is a religion of the soul which is concerned primarily with beauty and esthetics, such as beauty of form in architecture and music. It is very popular but it is a religion of the soul, concerned primarily with the emotions. But the Lord Jesus once said to the woman at the well of Samaria, *The hour is coming, and now is, when the true worshipers will worship the Father in spirit and truth, for such the Father seeks to worship him* (John 4:23). The only acceptable worship of God today has nothing at all to do with buildings, organs, vestments, choirs, candles and all the rest. These things may mean something to us, but not to God. The only acceptable worship to God is that worship which takes place in the spirit, the inner shrine, the inner man.

We enter this, the writer says, by the blood of Jesus. It is the only way in. It is important to remember what he has already taught us in this letter about the blood of Jesus. The blood of Jesus refers not merely to the blood of the man, Jesus, but in a very real sense, as we have already learned, it represents also our blood. Jesus was our representative, He died in our place, He was *made sin for us,* so that what happened to Him is what God sees as happening to us. This phrase, *the blood of Jesus,* is a symbolic way of saying that we must be willing to accept the sentence of death on the natural man, that we must die to our own ability to do anything for God of ourselves. That is what he is talking about. The only way into the realm of the spirit where God can be enjoyed face to face is by accepting that sentence of death upon the natural man. There is nothing that man, in himself, can offer to God, nothing that we can contribute, nothing that God finds pleasurable or favorable. To accept this is to enter into the value of the blood of Jesus. The only thing we can contribute to God is what He has first given us. And if we think otherwise we can never enter into this realm. Our worship will only be on the level of the soul and, as such, is unacceptable. But we have a way into the sanctuary. Our death, in Jesus, has opened that way. In His dying on the cross the Lord Jesus has torn the veil, that is, the flesh, so that the way into the inner shrine of man is wide open and we can freely enter. That is the first provision.

The second one is that we have a great Priest over the house of God. Remember what we have learned already in this letter as to what the house is. As the writer says distinctly in chapter 3, *whose house are we*[1] (v. 6). He is describing, then, the indwelling of Christ by the Spirit, the recognition of an indwelling Christ who offers to clothe Himself with our personality and is prepared to live His life over again in our circumstances, right where we are. This is the greatest truth of Christian faith. Christianity is not some feeble effort on our part to live a shabby imitation of Jesus Christ. Christianity is Jesus Christ living His life again through us right where we are, in our circumstances. We have a completely available and thoroughly able Priest in control over the house of God, whose house we are.

In Paul's letter to the Philippians, he says exactly the same thing. Writing to his dear friends in Philippi, he says, *We are the true circumcision, who worship God in spirit, and glory in Christ Jesus* [He is the one we count on], *and put no confidence in the flesh* [we have accepted God's sentence of death against the natural man] (Phil. 3:3). There is our complete provision: an awakened spirit and an adequate mediator.

Now, on that basis and that basis alone, the writer goes on to urge three things that we can do. Draw near, speak out, and stir up! Take the first, *Draw near with a true heart* (Heb. 10:22). If I may put that in more modern terms, he is saying that we are *to live continually in unfeigned dependence* upon an indwelling Christ. *Draw near* means continually to walk in the presence of God. You do not draw near to God when you come to church. You are no nearer to Him there than you are at work, at play, or wherever you are. If you have not learned how to draw near to Him in everyday life you will never learn how to draw near to Him in church. You draw near to God when you live in recognition of His presence in your life all the time. That is what He asks us to do.

When we draw near on that basis there are the wonderful results. First, *full assurance of faith.* That means living out of adequacy; that means to discover a source of supply which never runs dry. Your dependence is no longer upon the weak abilities you may have as a natural man: your talents, your gifts, your training, your education. Your dependence now is upon the flowing power of the Spirit of the living God who dwells in you, a river of living water, a supply that never runs dry. That is living out of adequacy. You are prepared to meet any circumstance, not in trepidation or trembling, but in the quiet confidence that He who is in you is able to do everything that needs to be done. That is full assurance, is it not? Full assurance of faith.

The second result of drawing near is *a heart sprinkled clean from an evil conscience.* There is freedom from guilt. How did you sleep last night? Were you restless, did you twist and turn? Were you troubled by an evil or guilty conscience? Perhaps a feeling of not having done the things you ought to have done? Psychologists tell us the whole race of man is suffering from a guilty conscience. This is the basic human problem, but Jesus Christ has come to meet that problem. The heart that comes before God on the terms outlined here experiences a complete freedom from the sense of nagging guilt. It is true peace. *You are accepted in the beloved*[1] (Eph. 1:6). Therefore you can be free from any undefined, nagging sense of guilt.

The third result is *our bodies washed with pure water* (Heb. 10:22). I can hear some saying "Amen" already, but unfortunately that phrase does not refer to baptism. There are some people who can find water baptism in every other verse of the Bible. Although it does mention water here, I am sure this is not a reference to water baptism, primarily because it makes particular reference to "pure water" and it is very difficult to get pure water for water baptism. I have baptized individuals in some very muddy streams which would make the rite invalid if this phrase referred to baptism. But this is again symbolic language, as is the rest of the verse. It refers to an outward life which has been cleansed, rearranged, changed by the new life in Christ. It means that thieves stop stealing, alcoholics stop drinking, liars stop lying, and sex sins come to an end. The whole life is changed because we have drawn near to God.

These are the things that are possible only as we approach on the basis outlined before: we come, accepting the sentence of death to all that is natural in us and depending on an indwelling Christ who is prepared to do through us everything that needs to be done.

But even this is but step number one in the possibilities of a Christian life. The second step to which we are urged is: *Let us hold fast the confession of our hope without wavering, for he who promised is faithful* (Heb. 10:23). That is, we are not only to draw near, but to speak out, to share the great secret. You can be confident that as you talk about what has happened to you, those who hear, acting upon the same basis as you acted, will experience the same results, for God is faithful. The One who has declared this, is no respecter of persons. He will do as much for the man next door as He has done for you; He will do as much for the boss at the top of the heap as He does for the man at the bottom. It makes no difference; He is faithful. Therefore you can rely upon the fact, in sharing what God has done in you, that He will do it also in someone else. Speak out, then. Hold fast the confession of your hope without wavering!

The third privilege is, *Let us consider how to stir up one another to love and good works, not neglecting to meet together, as is the habit of some, but encouraging one another, and all the more as you see the Day drawing near* (Heb. 10:24,25). How do you stir someone up to love and good works? These two things are always the mark of true Christianity. Christians are never judged by the confessions they make or the creed they recite; it is always by their deeds. How much practical love have you manifested? How far have you responded to the cry for help from someone near you, someone who is destitute or disappointed, who needs an encouraging word or a helping hand or a generous check? This is the ultimate test.

Well, how do you achieve this? The writer suggests two ways. First, by not neglecting to meet together. That is very important. "Not neglecting to meet together . . . but encouraging one another." That suggests the character of the meetings. They are not to be discouraging meetings, they are to be encouraging meetings. They are to be meetings where you can hear again the tremendous, radical principles of Christian faith, and see again in human lives the mighty power of the One whom we worship and serve, and where you can understand how God works through human society, how He is transforming and changing men everywhere. To thus meet together is to encourage one another in these things. That is what Christian services ought to be like: to hear the Word of God so that it comes home with power to the heart, and to share with one another the results. If our services were more like this we would not have trouble in getting people to come out. Too often church services are the kind pictured in the story of the father who was showing his son through a church building. They came to a plaque on the wall and the little boy asked, "Daddy, what's that for?" His father said, "Oh, that's a memorial to those who died in the service." The little boy said, "Which service, Daddy, the morning service or the evening service?" Meetings of Christians are to be essentially encouraging things, and this is one way we stir up one another to love and good works.

The second way is a watchful awareness of the time, *all the more as you see the Day drawing near. The Day* is the certain return of Jesus Christ. As evil becomes more subtle, as it becomes more and more difficult to tell the difference between truth and error, good and bad, right and wrong; as the clamant voices of our age pour out deceitful lies and we find the whole of society permeated and infiltrated with false concepts that deny the truth of the Word of God, we need all the more to gather together and encourage one another by sharing the secrets of life in Christ Jesus. You have the privilege of all three of these, draw near, speak out, stir up: that is the whole Christian life in a nutshell. This is a privilege open to everyone, if you come on the proper basis. The only reason they escape you is because you have not come by the way outlined at the beginning of this passage. And be very careful! Do not take this lightly. For in the next section the writer flashes a red light of warning.

He goes on to speak of a presumption which invites punishment.

For if we sin deliberately after receiving the knowledge of the truth, there no longer remains a sacrifice for sins, but a fearful prospect of judgment, and a fury of fire which will consume the adversaries. A man who has violated the law of Moses dies without mercy at the testimony of two or three witnesses. How much worse punishment do you think will be deserved by the man who has spurned the Son of God, and profaned

the blood of the covenant by which he was sanctified, and outraged the Spirit of grace? For we know him who said, "Vengeance is mine, I will repay." And again, "The Lord will judge his people." It is a fearful thing to fall into the hands of the living God.
(Heb. 10:26-31).

What a somber passage! What is this willful, deliberate sin that has such terrible results? The tense of the word indicates immediately that this is not a single act of folly or weakness. This is not something one can stumble into suddenly. It is not the normal falterings of a Christian who is still learning how to walk in the Spirit. None of these is in view at all. The continuous present tense of this wording, "sin deliberately," marks a long-continued attitude of resistance. It is, of course, the sin the writer has warned against all along in Hebrews. It is the sin of knowing the principle of the denial of self in following Christ, and a consistent refusal to do so. I ran across a startling phrase that beautifully expresses this. It is "the leukemia of noncommitment." It is refusing to cease from our own works and enter into God's rest, refusing the cross in our life. It is choosing to live for self behind a Christian veneer, refusing the claims of the Lordship of Jesus Christ.

This is not possible when this new arrangement for living is not yet clearly understood. I want that to be clear. This willful sin is never the sin of ignorance. It is a presumptuous choice of self-living when we know perfectly well, from the Word of God, what the results of that choice will be. What the writer is saying here is that once that choice has been fully made (and by the grace of God this may take years), then there is no way back. It is exactly the same situation faced in Hebrews 6. There is certain judgment ahead, the writer says, *a fearful prospect of judgment, and a fury of fire which will consume the adversaries.* He argues from the less to the greater. If this were true even under the shadows of the law; if, when a man violated even these pictures of Christ and His work, he suffered death at the mouth of two or three witnesses, how much more shall he be culpable if he violates knowingly and deliberately the reality which is Jesus Christ?

This kind of sin, the writer goes on to point out, always involves three things. There is first a spurning of the Son of God. He deliberately chooses a title for Jesus which emphasizes His right to be Lord over life, *the Son of God.* There is a consistent spurning of that, a refusal to buckle under, to acknowledge Christ's right to govern the life. And there is also a profaning of the blood of Christ. That means a rejection of the principle referred to earlier, a refusal of the sentence of death that God has pronounced upon the natural life. It is presuming to approve what God condemns. It is to insist that our efforts to serve God ought to be accepted by Him, even though He has said they are not acceptable. It is to insist that our religious activities ought to be enough, when God has said these things have all been set aside in the death of Christ. That is profaning the blood by which we are sanctified. Then the third thing, the most serious of all, is the outraging of the Spirit of grace. This is to treat with indifference (and indifference is always the cruelest form of hate) the pleadings, wooings, and leadings of the Spirit of God. It is to insult the Holy Spirit. This, then, is the dread "blasphemy against the Holy Ghost," for which Jesus said there is no forgiveness, neither in this age nor in the world to come.

I am often asked, "Can Christians commit the blasphemy against the Holy Spirit?" The answer is both "yes" and "no." Christians who have declared that, come hell or high water, sink or swim, live or die, their only hope is the promise of Christ; who, when they find themselves sinning and failing, own up and return to Christ and trust Him again, that kind of Christian can never commit the blasphemy against the Holy Ghost. They are "born of God" and can never do this. But Christians who sin and do nothing about it, who resent the Lordship of Jesus Christ, who resist His authority and do as they please regardless of what the Word of God says, that kind of Christian is in grave danger of this very thing. That is why this letter was written. Such prove themselves to be "embryo Christians," as we saw in Hebrews 6, never truly born of God. They have entered into the initiatory relationship of the Christian life by the Holy Spirit but never pass on to that taking of the yoke of Christ upon them that means a new birth. That kind can drift into this dangerous position.

To put yourself into the hands of the living Christ; to trust Him and obey Him; to believe that He is the truth and you mean therefore to follow Him and do what He says, that is a glorious thing.

"The hands of Christ are very frail
For they were broken with a nail,

But only those reach Heaven at last
Whom those frail,
broken hands hold fast."

It is one thing to put yourself into the hands of the living Christ; but to fall into the hands of the living God, when you have professed one thing but have consistently, deliberately refused to obey it, that is quite another thing. The writer says, "It is a fearful thing to fall into the hands of the living God." We greatly need these words of warning. There is a cursed, superficial concept of God abroad today that is doing great damage to many. It is the idea of a palsy-walsy God who slaps you on the back and says, "Everything is fine, don't worry about a thing, I'm with you to the end no matter what you do." God has never revealed Himself like that. His self-revelation is continually other than this. The God whom we worship can be to us the very dearest person in the universe. He offers to be dearer and closer and more wonderful than any earthly friend can possibly be, but only on terms which, in His wisdom and grace, He has seen are absolutely necessary to make that relationship a permanent one. On any other terms He is not available.

There is not one of us who would dare defy the laws of chance by endlessly playing Russian roulette. We would know that sooner or later the laws of chance would catch up with us and we would be gone. If we were killed it would be our own fault. Well then, shall we defy the living God and think we can escape? This is what the author asks.

During the Vietnam conflict the front page of the

local paper one day had a picture of a man with a revolver in his hand standing over the crumpled body of a Vietnamese soldier. Underneath was the title, "The Price of Defection." The soldier was a traitor. This is what the writer describes in Hebrews: traitors to the cause they espouse. They say they are obeying Christ, but they consistently refuse to walk in His steps.

Now I know the question that is on your heart. It is, "How can I know whether I am one of these?" And the answer is in this last section. There is here described a fortitude which reveals faith.

But recall the former days when, after you were enlightened, you endured a hard struggle with sufferings, sometimes being publicly exposed to abuse and affliction, and sometimes being partners with those so treated. For you had compassion on the prisoners, and you joyfully accepted the plundering of your property, since you knew that you yourselves had a better possession and an abiding one. Therefore do not throw away your confidence, which has a great reward. For you have need of endurance, so that you may do the will of God and receive what is promised. "For yet a little while, and the coming one shall come and shall not tarry; but my righteous one shall live by faith, and if he shrinks back, my soul has no pleasure in him." But we are not of those who shrink back and are destroyed, but of those who have faith and keep their souls.
(Heb. 10:32-39).

In these words the author recognizes that most of

these to whom he writes had already given proof of true faith and genuine birth. Their early Christian years were marked by love and joy and hope, despite hardships and persecution. They had followed Christ at cost to themselves. They had submitted themselves to the Lordship of Christ, even when their own will would have been different. That is the mark of reality, the proof of faith. They cheerfully and compassionately accepted the persecutions, deprivations and hardships that came their way. They took Christ's yoke upon themselves, obeyed His Lordship, and manifested it by love and good works. They were living by faith. You can do these things only when you live by faith. When you have accepted God's Word and recognized that Christ is who He says He is, and that the history of the world is going to turn out as He says it is, and that the values of life are what He says they are, then and then only can you do this kind of thing.

Now they need to do only one more thing–keep on! That is all. They are doing the right thing. The road will end at the dawning of a new day and the coming of the living God. Does your way sometimes seem hard and difficult? Is it, perhaps, often lonely and exposed to the reproach of others? Well, do not despair; do not give up. That pattern has been predicted; that is part of Christian living today, as it has always been. For if you live by faith, if you accept what this Word says as true and you see that it is working out in history exactly as God said it would; if you are counting on His strength to bring about all that He promises; if you thus live by faith, then, though it be through scourgings and mockings, through perils and dangers, you will arrive, for "the just shall live by faith." That is the great sentence that burned in the heart of Martin Luther and lit the fires of the Reformation: "The just shall live by faith." Not by circumstances, not by outward appearances, but by faith in what the Word of God has declared. You need only to continue to endure to reach the goal.

Faith could well be translated, in modern parlance, by the word "toughness." In chapter 11, we shall see some illustrations of men and women who have lived by faith. These are the tough people of history. They have endured, they have toughed it out, they have stuck it out. They faced all the pressures, all the problems, all the confusing duplicity of life, but because they had their eye fixed on One who never changes they were tough—nothing could move them aside or divert them. Now that is what the apostle is calling for, that inner toughness which meets life steadfastly, unmovably, unshakably, is never driven off its position of faith. It constantly meets every encounter, every challenge by resting upon the Word of God, relying upon what God said would take place. God grant that we may find that toughness in these terrible and glorious days.

"Our Father, this has been a solemn passage we have looked at together, but we thank You for the truth which dares to speak even though it offends. We thank You, Lord, for the love which tells us the truth though it hurts. Keep us from the utter folly of taking these words and rationalizing them in some foolish manipulation that destroys their meaning. Give us the grace to be honest with You, to look at ourselves earnestly and honestly and to ask ourselves where we stand, and by Your grace, Lord, to lay hold of this marvelous way of deliverance, to yield the total man into the control of the total Lordship of Jesus Christ.
We pray in His name,
Amen."

11

what faith is

The eleventh chapter of Hebrews is one of the best known of the great chapters of the Bible. It has been called the "Westminster Abbey of Scripture" because the heroes of faith are enshrined here. Perhaps that is a misnomer, for I have been in Westminster Abbey and it gave me the sense of being in a tomb. There are a lot of dead people there but there are no dead people in this chapter. These are all living saints, triumphant men and women who have lived life and gone on into a new relationship. I prefer, then, to call this "The Parade of the Heroes of Faith."

In Hebrews there is an element which is regarded as absolutely essential to the development of the Christian life, and that is the quality of faith. It is what makes the Christian different from the non-Christian. That rather eccentric philosopher and nature lover of New England in the last century, Henry David Thoreau, once said, "If I seem to walk out of step with others, it is because I am listening to another drum beat." That is an exact description of faith: Christians walk as though listening to another drum beat.

This chapter centers on and focuses upon what faith is. There is need for clarity on this. I find this word, faith, is greatly misunderstood and there are many peculiar ideas of what it is. It might help to show, first of all, what faith is not. Faith, for instance, is not positive thinking; that is something quite different. Faith is not a hunch that is followed. Faith is not hoping for the best, hoping that everything will turn out all right. Faith is not a feeling of optimism. Faith is none of these things though all of them have been identified as faith.

Well, what is faith then? The first seven verses of this wonderful chapter answer that question, and the rest of the chapter tells us how it works. We will limit our thought to these first seven verses now. The author is not discussing faith, in general, but faith in God. If this is important, then it is essential that we know what it is.

In these seven verses there is a definition in which we see the ingredients of faith. This, by the way, is the only definition of faith in the Bible. The definition is followed by a deduction, in which we have revealed the significance, the implications, of faith. Then there is a demonstration, in which we see illustrations of faith. The first and second verses and the sixth verse, taken together, help define faith for us. Here we see the ingredients of faith.

Now faith is the assurance of things hoped for, the conviction of things not seen. For by it the men of

old received divine approval. . . . And without faith it is impossible to please God. For whoever would draw near to God must believe that he exists and that he rewards those who seek him.
(Heb. 11:1,2,6).

Note how those verses indicate that faith begins with hope. Faith commences with things hoped for, that is, it starts with a sense of discontent. You can never have much faith unless you are dissatisfied with the way you are now and are longing for something better. That is its first note. If you do not feel dissatisfied with the way you are it will be impossible for you to exercise any faith. That is why, all through the Bible, the great enemy of faith is a complacent spirit, an attitude of self-satisfaction with the status quo. But if you are dissatisfied, if you are looking for something better, if you are not content to be merely a cultured animal living out a life of eating, sleeping and amusing yourself and eventually dying, then you are in a position to exercise faith. Someone has described that kind of life this way:

"Into this world to eat and to sleep
And to know no reason why he was born
Save to consume the corn
Devour the cattle, flock and fish
And leave behind an empty dish."

Perhaps there are many who would like to have faith but are never ready for it because they are not dissatisfied. They must demand of life more than the mere mechanics of living. You want more, do you not? You are looking for something better? Then that is the first note of faith. Verse 6 puts it, *he who would draw near to God.* That is, looking for more of life than is visible on the surface. Such a one is not satisfied to have life all surface, all length and breadth, but no depth. He wants to find something to deepen life, and that is the first note of faith.

Then comes *the conviction of things not seen.* Not only a desire for something better, but an awareness of something else. That is faith. It means we become aware that we are surrounded by an invisible spiritual kingdom, that which is seen is not the whole explanation of life, that there are realities which cannot be seen, weighed, measured, analyzed, or touched, and yet which are as real and as vital as anything we can see. In fact they are more real because they are the explanation of things which can be seen. We must understand there is a spiritual kingdom that exists. This is so beautifully seen in the words and teachings of our Lord Jesus. He speaks of God the Father as though He were standing right there, invisible and yet present. He speaks of the world as a great family home in which there is a Father with a Father's heart welcoming us. He does not see the universe as an impersonal machine, grinding and clanking along, as science so frequently does, but He sees it as an invisible, but very real, spiritual kingdom.

Again verse 6 says the same. *He that comes to God must believe that He is, that God exists.* There are some who say, "That's the hard part, that's what is difficult." No, it is not. The easiest thing in the world to do is to believe God exists. It requires effort to disbelieve; it requires no effort to believe. The interesting thing is that everyone in the world, without exception, starts out believing God exists. It is only when they are carefully trained to disbelieve that they come to the place of declaring God does not exist. Light from God is streaming in on every side and all we need to do is open our eyes to see it and know that God is there. That is why children have no problem with this. The concept of God ought to be one of the most difficult ideas for children to grasp, since God cannot be seen. But the amazing thing is that children have no difficulty at all in believing that God exists.

It requires long and careful effort to train the mind to reject this evidence and explain it on other terms. Some time ago I skimmed through Julian Huxley's book, *Religion Without Revelation,* and was amazed again to see the tremendous effort he makes to explain away the evidence for the existence of God, and to find other explanations for it. It is only those minds, therefore, that have deliberately trained themselves that can claim to be atheistic. Even then, if they are not careful, they may suddenly refer to a belief in God, as the man who on one occasion exclaimed, "I'm an atheist, thank God!"

There is also a third ingredient of faith, "the assurance of things hoped for." Faith is the assurance that the things hoped for, the things you are longing to have, the better man or woman you would like to be, will be achieved by reliance on the things unseen. Let us put it all together now. It begins with a longing to be something better, and an awareness that within the universe there is something else, and that something or Someone else has revealed itself. As we act on that revelation we shall achieve the things hoped for, the something better. That is the story of the whole eleventh chapter of Hebrews; it is the story of faith. It will work for anyone at any level.

Here, by the way, is the answer to that persistent question we so frequently face, "What about the heathen who never hear the gospel?" They have the opportunity to exercise faith, for faith at its simplest level is, *Whoever would draw near to God must believe that He exists and that He rewards those who seek Him.* Any man who wants to be better, who believes that God exists and who will obey the revelation that he has, no matter at whatever level he finds it, expecting God to give him more as he goes along, will come to the place where he wins divine approval, the place of knowing Jesus Christ. Without that faith it is impossible to please God.

Verse 3 introduces us to a very amazing deduction which reveals something of the significance of faith, the implications of it. *By faith we understand that the world was created by the word of God, so that what is seen was made out of things which do not appear.*

That statement, remember, was made in the first century when the best scientific minds of the time felt that the ultimate breakdown of matter was fourfold: fire, water, soil and air. That was the explanation of all matter. Yet here in the twentieth century, after two thousand years of human endeavor in exploring the secrets of the origin of matter, we cannot improve on this statement. This verse says that we can never explain the things which are seen till we come to grips with the things that are unseen. We must

The first is Abel.

By faith Abel offered to God a more acceptable sacrifice than Cain, through which he received approval as righteous, God bearing witness by accepting his gifts; he died, but through his faith he is still speaking. (Heb. 11:4).

Here are the world's first brothers, Abel and Cain, sons of Adam and Eve. They lived when the world was young, when everything was much different than it is today. It was before the days of income tax and smog and clogged highways and the terrible problems that we struggle with. Yet, despite the fact that they enjoyed what we call "the simple life," they longed for something better, they hungered after God. For no matter how good life is, it is never good enough if you do not have God. Man is never satisfied without Him, and these boys hungered for God. Both had been told the way by which they could come to Him; this is implied in the account. But Cain chose to believe a lie, the lie that is still very evident today, that "one way is as good as another." He took the way that was easiest for him to work out and as a result he was rejected; for, of course, it is always a lie that one way is as good as another. That never works in anything–nature, life, or with God.

But Abel believed God and came the way God had outlined. When he believed God he discovered a great truth, the truth that man cannot have God's ability until he is prepared to recognize the poverty of his own. That is what a blood sacrifice teaches. There must be a life laid down before one can have the life of God. You cannot have His ability for your problems until you are first ready to lay aside any dependence upon your own ability. That is the greatest truth that man can ever learn. If we learn that here, as some of us are learning it, what a difference it makes in life! Because Abel was the first man to learn that truth, the writer says he is still speaking to us–and we still need to listen!

Then there is Enoch. Enoch was the seventh man from Adam.

By faith Enoch was taken up so that he should not see death; and he was not found, because God had taken him. Now before he was taken he was attested as having pleased God.
(Heb. 11:5).

In the book of Genesis we are told that for sixty-five years this man lived like anyone else in his day, no different from the rest of his age. But at the age of sixty-five, something happened. It was not that he got his Social Security–he found a deeper security than that. The record says he began to walk with God; he began for the first time to enjoy the continuous presence of an unseen Person, and he related his life daily to that unseen Person who was with him. When he did that he discovered a great reality, just as you will if you try it. He found a fellowship that death could not interrupt. According to the record, he never died. He was one of two men in the Scriptures of whom it is recorded that they never died. He was "not found," that is all. God took him, the record says, without death.

I love the way the little Sunday School girl told it. She said, "Enoch was a man who learned to walk with God, and they used to take long walks together. One day they walked so far that God said, 'Look, Enoch, it's too far for you to go back; just come on home with Me.' So he walked on home with God." He became forever a picture of what death is to the Christian–only an incident, hardly worth mentioning. That is the reality that Enoch discovered by faith.

Then there is Noah. Noah believed God in a unique way.

By faith Noah, being warned by God concerning events as yet unseen, took heed and constructed an ark for the saving of his household; by this he condemned the world and became an heir of the righteousness which comes by faith.
(Heb. 11:7).

Noah believed that God was in control of history. All the things these men believed we are asked to believe today; there is no difference. Noah believed that God was in charge of history. He believed when God told him there was coming a great flood. When Noah told this around everyone began to laugh and say how foolish he was. But Noah went right ahead and built a boat. Now that is not unusual in these days, but he built it five hundred miles from the nearest ocean, a thousand times too big for his own family, and when he got it finished he filled it with animals! I am sure I know what they called Noah in those days: "Nutty Noah." But he anticipated history and thus showed how shortsighted the world is when it walks in the light of its own reason. He was led on by his faith to become *an heir of the righteousness which comes by faith*—that is, faith in Christ Jesus—and he became part of the divine family. That is what faith is: acting on what God says.

Faith is believing there is another dimension to life other than those which can be touched, tasted, seen or felt. There is more to life than that. There is also the realm of the spirit, the invisible spiritual Kingdom of God. All the ultimate answers of life lie in that kingdom. Faith believes that God, in His grace, has stepped over the boundary into human history and told us some great and very valuable facts. Faith believes them and adjusts its life to those facts and walks on that basis. The world does not understand, and often uses derogatory terms for those who walk by faith. Certainly they are not oddballs in every way, although in some ways every Christian is; but though the world does not understand why, the man who walks by faith wins the day because he has come in touch with things as they really are. That is the glory of faith.

Now do you have faith? Are you a man or woman of faith? Is there a hunger for something better in your life? Is there a conviction that God is ready to answer your cry? In fact, He has already answered it, in Christ! Are you ready then to commit yourself to obey what He says, to accept His verdict, His viewpoint, as the true one despite the clamant cries that will pour into your ear from every side, saying this is wrong? That is what faith is, and if you are that kind of a man or woman you can join this parade of faith in this unfinished chapter.

I read an account of a dear Christian woman in Africa who died, and the village gathered to pay its respects at the funeral. There were many kind things said about her, but one of the most revealing was the comment, "If the Bible is going to be rewritten in heaven, this woman ought to be in it." Now the Bible is not going to be rewritten in heaven. It never needs to be rewritten for it is truth, and truth never needs to change. But one thing will happen to it. There are certain sections of it that will be extended because they are unfinished–the book of Acts, for instance, and the eleventh chapter of Hebrews. We are still following the same program. God is still calling men and women to live by faith. And if by faith in what God has said we conduct our lives according to this revelation, we too shall someday have our names added to this parade of the heroes of faith, the men and women who have done the only great things the world has ever really known.

"Our Father, thank You for this glimpse into the life of the past and this revelation of what faith is today. How we feel the need of it in this hour, as we live in the midst of a confused and bewildered society, a world that is troubled, uncertain, unstable, in the grip of lies that it thinks are truths, and rejecting truths that it regards as lies. God, grant us the simple faith of a child by which we can trust Your love, trust Your word, and believe You have told us the truth. Teach us to live according to it, coming to know Jesus Christ our living Lord, by whom life can be changed and all that we hope for may be realized. Though it be through difficulties, through trials, through heartache and tears, yet we shall win the day, we shall arrive at the goal, we shall be what we long to be, in Him.
For His sake,
Amen."

12

how faith works

Once I attended two graduation exercises for local schools. At each, able young orators with admirable self-assurance told us what was wrong with the world and what improvements we can expect when their generation takes control. Behind all the truly fine words there was evident one philosophy. It was that the human mind, educated to a high degree, was, in its collective manifestation, a completely adequate instrument with which to solve human problems. Now the writer of Hebrews challenges that philosophy head-on. He says that man's reason, operating alone, invariably misinterprets the evidence, and that it was never intended so to operate; that reason is a beautiful instrument designed of God and excellently suited for the realm in which it was intended to operate, but that man's reason, as it exists now, is deprived of an essential dimension of life. That missing dimension is an absolutely necessary ingredient if we ever expect to solve our problems.

The writer goes on to point out, as we have been

seeing all along, that God has spoken to man and has revealed basic truths about life. That revelation is quite different from what man's unaided reason feels is the explanation of secrets of living. If we accept the revelation and act on these truths (that is what faith is, accepting and acting on them), reason then will find its proper place and life will make sense as God intended it to do. But without faith we only struggle on in a confused cycle of bewilderment, boredom and frustration.

The writer has made clear that the revelation of God all centers in Jesus Christ; therefore the life of faith begins by an acceptance of Him. Faith, as we have already seen, is a desire for something better. It starts with hope. Then it is an awareness of Someone else in life, an unseen Someone who is nevertheless very real. Then faith involves an assurance that obedience to that Someone will bring us to the something better. Faith, therefore, is a very practical thing, is it not? The writer is well aware that a living illustration always helps, hence this mighty eleventh chapter which is filled with the simple stories of men and women of like passion with ourselves, living in the kind of a world in which we live, confronted with the same kind of problems, who mastered their problems and overcame the obstacles and won their way to tremendous fulfillment by faith. This chapter hardly needs exposition, as these accounts are self-explanatory; but perhaps it may be helpful to point out five outstanding characteristics of faith manifested in this eleventh chapter. You can test your own faith by these, for here are the distinguishing marks of genuine faith.

Perhaps the most characteristic thing is that faith always anticipates; it moves toward a clearly expected event in the future. It was Soren Kierkegaard, the Danish philosopher, who said, "Life can only be understood backwards, but it must be lived forward." With that fact none can quarrel. But without faith, life must perforce be a blind march into mystery. We cannot know where we are going, we do not know what is coming, we do not see what lies ahead. The future is an imponderable enigma to those without faith; anything can happen. Therefore there is always a sense of anxiety in trying to look ahead. But faith believes that God has revealed something about the future; not everything, but something. And what He has revealed is quite enough for us to know. Faith seizes upon a revealed event and begins to live in anticipation of it. Therefore, faith gives to life goal, purpose and destination. It is a look into the future.

See this in Abraham. We are told in verse 9, *By faith he sojourned in the land of promise.* He dwelt there, living in tents with Isaac and Jacob who were heirs with him of the promises, because *he looked forward to the city which has foundations, whose builder and maker is God* (v. 10). Here is an illustration of the meaninglessness of time in the life of faith. It is amazing how far Abraham saw. As best we can tell, Abraham lived about two thousand years before Christ. We live about two thousand years after Him. Yet Abraham, looking forward by faith, believing what God had said would take place, looked across these forty centuries of time and beyond to the day when God would bring to pass on earth a city with eternal foundations; that is, life on earth would be lived after God's order. Abraham saw what John sees in the book of Revelation, a city coming down out of heaven onto earth. I think that is a symbol—perhaps it is a literal city—but I think it is symbolic of that for which we pray in the Lord's Prayer: *Thy will be done on earth as it is in heaven.* That is what Abraham longed for, an earth run after God's order, where men would dwell together in peace, harmony, blessing, beauty and fulfillment. Because of that, he was content to dwell in tents, looking for that coming.

You can see this quality of anticipation also in Isaac, Jacob and Joseph. Isaac and Jacob both knew that God intended to make nations from their sons, and their final prayers were based upon that fact. They prayed in anticipation of what God had said would come, and blessed their children on that basis. Joseph, when he was dying, saw two hundred years ahead to the coming exodus from Egypt, and he made arrangements by faith for a funeral service in the Promised Land. He did not want to be buried in Egypt. Thus he symbolized his conviction that God was going to do exactly as He had said. And in the course of time it happened exactly that way.

You can see how faith anticipates in the case of Moses' parents who, when he was born, saw that he was a beautiful child, a *goodly child* (Exod. 2:2) and they decided to save him from the edict of the king that all male children should be slain. This was more than the natural desire of parents to preserve their children (even an especially handsome child like Moses) from death. But these parents knew there was a promise of deliverance from Egypt for their people, and they knew that the time was near. God had foretold how long it would be. They were given assurance that this boy was to be the deliverer. They believed that promise and, acting on that, they defied the king and hid the child for three months.

Related to this quality of faith which accepts as certain a promise of the future is a second quality, that faith always *acts*. There is today a very common misconception that thinks of men and women of faith as so occupied with the future that they sit around, twiddling their thumbs, doing nothing *now*. A very trite saying describes these types: "So heavenly-minded they are no earthly good." That unfortunately is the common concept of faith. But that is not faith; that is fatalism! Faith works! Faith is doing something now, in view of the future. If you are folding your hands and waiting for the Second Coming you are not living the life of faith. The life of faith is that which will *occupy till I come*, as Jesus said. It acts now in view of that coming event.

Take each example in this chapter and you will see that it is one of action. Without exception these men and women were set to work by their faith. Their faith made them act in the present. Therefore faith is not passive, it is dynamic, forceful. Listen to the magnificent summary here of the actions of faith.

And what more shall I say? For time would fail me to tell of Gideon, Barak, Samson, Jephthah, of David and Samuel and the prophets—who through faith conquered kingdoms, enforced justice, received promises, stopped the mouths of lions, quenched raging fire, escaped the edge of the sword, won strength out of weakness, became mighty in war, put foreign armies

to flight. Women received their dead by resurrection. Some were tortured, refusing to accept release, that they might rise again to a better life.
(Heb. 11:32-35).

That is not poetry; that is history—faith at work. The activities of faith have changed the course of history. Yet faith does not act blindly, either; it is not doing just anything. It is made very clear in this chapter that faith evaluates, it weighs the possibilities, the alternatives. Perhaps we could just as accurately put it, faith risks! One characteristic of faith is that it gladly sacrifices present advantage in order to gain the future. It does not try to have its cake and eat it too. Therefore, it clashes head-on with the common philosophy of our day, "Get it now or you may never have another chance."

The Stanford *Daily* carried a recent ad in response to some earlier advertisements put in by a fine group called Contemporary Christians on Campus. This recent ad originated with a group who signed themselves Contemporary Atheists on Campus. It said in flaming letters, "Deny God now; tomorrow may be too late." There is an ironic truth about that, but the message they intended to convey was that it was necessary to lay hold of the present *now* because at the end of life one may find there is no God and no after-life and thus lose all opportunity to invest oneself in worthwhile enterprises now. That was their argument.

But do you see how faith contravenes that? Faith says exactly the opposite. These heroes of faith say to us, live now in view of the future, and you will gain both the future and the present! Fling away the temporary now and you will both gain the future and, to your own amazement, find that the present has taken on fulness of meaning. It is given back to you, again and again.

You can see this in Abraham. We read,

By faith Abraham obeyed when he was called to go out to a place which he was to receive as an inheritance; and he went out, not knowing where he was to go.
(Heb. 11:8).

That is rather unusual. Here is a man who left home and went abroad without making any reservations. He went out on a march without a map, leaving his friends and his influence behind. There must have been many who said to him, "What an absurd thing to do, to go out not knowing where you are going. What is your destination?" And Abraham said, "I don't know." He did not know where he was going, but he knew *whom* he was going with, and what a difference that makes. Because he obeyed, the land became his and his children's. Even to this twentieth-century hour we have ample evidence in the existence of the nation Israel in that very same land that the promise God made to Abraham is valid, forty centuries later.

You can see how faith weighs and evaluates in the example of Moses. We are told that Moses,

when he was grown up, refused to be called the son

of Pharaoh's daughter, choosing rather to share ill-treatment with the people of God than to enjoy the fleeting pleasures of sin.
(Heb. 11:24,25).

He weighed the wealth of Egypt and the prestige of royalty against the satisfaction of being an instrument of the living God and an heir of the promises of God. He unhesitatingly chose because, we are told, he saw the unseen; he looked beyond the visible and saw the Invisible and believed in Him. He saw God at work and because of that, Moses became the man, more than any other man in recorded history, who saw God doing things and learned to know God intimately.

You can see faith evaluating in the case of Rahab, the prostitute. She risked her life and forsook her pagan religion. Why? Because she believed in God and thus she saved her life and her family's, and she gained God as well. Faith is never something merely for the future, but faith says that if we invest in that future which God offers us, we shall gain both the future and the present.

There is another summary in verse 36,

Others suffered mocking and scourging, and even chains and imprisonment. They were stoned, they were sawn in two, they were killed with the sword; they went about in skins of sheep and goats, destitute, afflicted, ill-treated–of whom the world was not worthy–wandering over deserts and mountains, and in dens and caves of the earth.
(Heb. 11:36-38).

But perhaps the most striking quality of all is that faith dares. When God has spoken, faith ignores the contrary evidence even though it seems to be absolutely impossible. Look at Abraham and Sarah in verses 11 and 12.

By faith Sarah herself received power to conceive, even when she was past the age, since she considered him faithful who had promised. Therefore from one man, and him as good as dead, were born descendants as many as the stars of heaven and as the innumerable grains of sand by the seashore.
(Heb. 11:11,12).

Here were two people, a man and his wife, whose bodies were impotent. They had long since passed the age of childbearing. He was a hundred, she was ninety; there is not a gynecologist alive who would give them a chance to have a child—but they went ahead, anyway. And the result was one little boy from whom came two lines of descendants, the writer tells us, a heavenly seed and an earthly seed. The earthly seed, the physical seed of Abraham, is the nation of Israel. The heavenly seed are those who show the same kind of faith that Abraham did and win the gift of righteousness by faith, as Paul says in Romans 4. That heavenly seed includes many who are presently reading this, who have found Jesus Christ, the Seed of Abraham, and thus have become children of Abraham.

You can see the daring of faith in Abraham again when he offered Isaac. Think of that! His reason could see no solution to his problem. God had said to him,

"Through this boy Isaac your descendants will be named." And now God was telling him to take the boy out and put him to death. Reason could never figure that out, but Abraham was not walking by reason but by faith. He believed that God had a solution to that problem, though man could not solve it. He believed God would raise the boy from the dead, if need be, to fulfill His promise; so thoroughly did Abraham believe that God meant what He said. As a result we have this amazing account of how Abraham, as it were, received the boy back from the dead, for in Abraham's mind he was as good as dead. But his faith triumphed and God gave him back the boy.

You can see the daring of faith in the people of Israel at the Red Sea and before the walls of Jericho. Here were two impossibilities. The waters were flowing before them and God said to go down and walk through it. They obeyed, not knowing what God would do. It was impossible from an earthly standpoint, but as they went forward God moved the waters back by a great wind and they went through on dry land. The Egyptians, trying to do it without faith, drowned. When the great walls of Jericho stood before them, 85 feet thick and over 100 feet high, impassable, impossible, they had only feeble instruments of warfare; but in obedience to God they marched around the city seven times and the walls fell down. By an earthquake, you say? Yes, perhaps so, but it was an earthquake that came in God's time and in God's place, and the walls were shaken down. Faith dares. It pays no attention to impossibilities. As someone has put it,

"Faith, mighty faith
The promise sees
And looks to God alone,
Laughs at impossibilities
And cries, 'It shall be done.' "

That brings us to the least spectacular but the most important aspect of faith. Faith persists, faith perseveres. Perhaps the most amazing statement in this amazing chapter is twice given. Though these people by faith obtained much from God, yet they all died without obtaining the promise they looked for.

These all died in faith, not having received what was promised, but having seen it and greeted it from afar, and having acknowledged that they were strangers and exiles on the earth. For people who speak thus make it clear that they are seeking a homeland. If they had been thinking of that land from which they had gone out, they would have had opportunity to return. But as it is, they desire a better country, that is, a heavenly one. Therefore God is not ashamed to be called their God, for he has prepared for them a city.
(Heb. 11:13-16).

They were looking for more than their own personal satisfaction. They were longing to see God's purposes fulfilled on earth. They were not just hoping to go to heaven when they died. These men and women of faith were looking for heaven to come to earth. They were looking to God to bring to pass His will among men, but they died without seeing it come to pass. There was a special reason for this.

And all these, though well attested by their faith, did not receive what was promised, since God had foreseen something better for us, that apart from us they should not be made perfect.
(Heb. 11:39,40).

Think back for a moment over the names in this chapter and what the world owes to these men and women. Noah, Abraham, Moses, David, and the prophets. Our laws, our governments, our institutions, our ideals, and our standards we owe to these men and women. They persisted in faith till the whole world was blessed. Had they given up we would never have heard of them. But still they did not see the greatest thing of all, and the reason was that God had arranged it that we, living in this twentieth century, might share this race and have a part in the great prize for which they were looking. We are called to run the same race. We are called to judge the present by the future, to weigh the permanent against the temporary, the ephemeral. To dare to do the impossible against all the silken arguments of the world around about us and to keep on day after day after day, whether we are recognized or not.

Now the whole great argument of this chapter is lost if we do not read the first verses of chapter 12.

Therefore, since we are surrounded by so great a cloud of witnesses, let us also lay aside every weight, and sin which clings so closely, and let us run with perseverance the race that is set before us, looking to Jesus the pioneer and perfecter of our faith, who for the joy that was set before him endured the cross,

despising the shame, and is seated at the right hand of the throne of God.
(vv. 1,2).

We are surrounded by a great cloud of witnesses, he says. Now that does not refer to people who have died and gone to heaven and are looking down on us from above. I know that is a favorite interpretation of this figure here, but I do not think that is what it means. It means that these people named in chapter 11 are saying something to us, they are testifying to us, they are witnesses in that sense. Their lives are saying that we ought to lay aside every weight, i.e., everything that hinders faith. You never say yes to Christ without saying no to something else! And the *sin which clings so closely*–what is that? That is unbelief. That is the failure to take revelation seriously. That is the sin which is mentioned all through Hebrews. And then what? *Run with patience, with perseverance, with persistence, keeping on no matter what happens.* How? By *looking unto Jesus,* that is the answer.

The others we read of here can inspire us and challenge us; and some of the men and women of faith who have lived since these days do the same. I read the life of Martin Luther, and what a challenge it is; and of John Wesley, and D. L. Moody, and of some of the recent martyrs of faith, Jim Elliot and others. How they have challenged my life and inspired me to make a fresh start; to determine anew to walk with God, and to follow their example. They challenge us to mobilize our resources, clench our fists, set our jaws and determine that we shall be men and women of faith in this twentieth century. But if that is our only motivation we shall find that we soon run out of gas. It all begins to fade and after a few weeks we are right back in the same old rut.

The secret of persistence is in this phrase, *looking unto Jesus.* The word means "looking away unto Jesus." Look at these men and women of faith, yes, but then look away unto Jesus. Why? Well, because He is the author and finisher of our faith. He can begin it and He can end it, complete it. He is the pioneer, He has gone on ahead. He is also the perfecter of faith. He Himself ran the race. He laid aside every weight, every tie of family and friends. Every restraining hand He brushed aside that He might resolutely walk with God. He set His face against the popular sin of unbelief and walked on in patient perseverance, trusting the Father to work everything out for Him. He set the example.

But there is more than example in this phrase; there is empowerment. That is what I want you to see. We are to look away unto Jesus because He can do what these others cannot do. They can inspire us, but He empowers us. Moment by moment, day by day, week by week, year by year, if we learn to look to Him we find strength imparted to us. That is the secret. You can find strength to begin in Jesus, you can venture out and start this life of faith today in Him. You also discover strength to continue. He is not "up there" somewhere. As this book has made clear, He is within us, by faith. If we have received Jesus Christ He dwells within. He has entered into the sanctuary, into the inner man, into the place where we need strength, and is available every moment for us–for me! Therefore, in Christ I have all that it takes to meet life. As Paul says, *I can do all things through Christ which strengtheneth me*[1] (Phil. 4:13).

"Our Father, thank You for a living Lord Jesus who, unlike these men and women of faith, is no distant person. He is not one that we cannot know and talk to, and draw strength from, and fellowship with, and lean upon. But He is our Lord, our living Lord, granted to the one who is ready to receive Him by a simple invitation and who is ready to trust Him through life to make available to us all that we need in every hour, whether of pressure or not. We thank You for this great truth. Teach us to live by it. In Christ's name,
Amen."

13

never give up

We are drawing now to the close of these studies in this great epistle of Christian life and liberty. The author of this letter has reviewed the exciting facts about Christian faith, and now in this twelfth chapter he comes to the practical exhortations that follow the presentation he has made. What he has to say is. "Never give up. You have started right," he says, "now hang on, never give up." It is all summarized in one verse. He says to these Christians then and to us now,

Consider him who endured from sinners such hostility against himself, so that you may not grow weary or fainthearted.
(Heb. 12:3).

That is the problem, is it not? Our tendency is to grow weary and to be fainthearted and slack off.

To get disinterested and live from day to day without much concern whether we are running the race of faith or not. This is the problem they had and it is the problem we face. This chapter stresses one great fact, the Christian life was never intended to be a picnic. It is bound to be rough, for it was rough for the Lord Jesus. *Consider him,* he says, *that endured such contradiction of sinners against himself.*[1] If you think it is hard living with the neighbors you live with, or working for the boss you work for, or living with mother-in-law you have to put up with, I suggest you review again the conditions our Lord faced in His earthly ministry. He had constantly to endure the stubbornness of men, the recalcitrant, obdurate attitude with which they refused to believe what He said. It was true even of His own disciples. How many times He had to rebuke them for being small in faith and even for putting stumbling blocks in the path of those who tried to come to Him. Again and again He endured the contradiction of sinners against Himself.

Now that is what the Christian life will be like, and we need to face it. Our Lord had to endure it clear to the end. It was He who reminded us that the servant is not greater than his master. If the world persecuted Him it will persecute us and if it kept His Word, it will keep our word as well. As Frances Ridley Havergal has reminded us,

> "God has not promised
> Skies always blue,
> Flower-strewn pathways
> All our life through."

The rest of the chapter enlarges upon this fact that the Christian life will include times of hardship and trials. In this chapter there are three reasons why these difficulties, disappointments and heartbreaks must come to us. First, trials manifest to us the discipline of love. Second, they allow opportunity for the demonstration of adequacy. Third, they expose to us the demarcation of truth. First there is a passage on the discipline of love.

In your struggle against sin you have not yet resisted to the point of shedding your blood. And have you forgotten the exhortation which addresses you as sons?— "My son, do not regard lightly the discipline of the Lord, nor lose courage when you are punished by him. For the Lord disciplines him whom he loves, and chastises every son whom he receives." It is for discipline that you have to endure. God is treating you as sons; for what son is there whom his father does not discipline? If you are left without discipline, in which all have participated, then you are illegitimate children and not sons.
(Heb. 12:4-8).

To these harassed, persecuted Christians, tempted (as we often are) with discouragement, the writer says, "Do not look at the dark side, look at the bright side; there is something good about discipline. First of all, it could be worse!" That is always encouraging, is it not? He reminds them, *You have not yet resisted to the point of shedding your blood; God has spared you what others have had to face. You should be grateful for that, for even the Son of God was not spared this.* Romans 8:32 reminds us, *He who did not spare his own Son but gave him up for us all, will he not also give us all things with him?*

Though we may have it rough, it has not been as rough as it could have been. The future may yet call for more strength on our part. When Jeremiah began to complain to the Lord about his problems, the Lord said to him, *If you have been running with the footmen and you find it difficult, what are you going to do when you compete with horses? And if you fall down when you are in a safe land, what will you do in the day of the swelling of Jordan?* (See Jer. 12:5, Author's Translation.) So God reminds us that even though trials come, they could be worse.

Second, hardships prove our sonship. Every boy knows that his father does not discipline the neighbor children, he disciplines him! The reason is that he is a son. God does not discipline the children of darkness either; He disciplines His own. Therefore, if we have discipline, if we are going through struggles and problems, then thank God. Even with our earthly fathers, he points out, we gave them respect during times of discipline.

Besides this, we have had earthly fathers to discipline us and we respected them. Shall we not much more be subject to the Father of spirits and live? For they disciplined us for a short time at their pleasure, but he disciplines us for our good, that we may share his holiness.
(Heb. 12:9,10).

"At their pleasure" does not mean that fathers whip

their children in order to amuse themselves; it means they did what they thought was right, though sometimes they were wrong. Every young person can say "Amen" to that! But God is never wrong. What He does is right. What He sends is exactly what we need; He is never wrong. God loves us and He sends exactly what we need; that is the argument here.

One definition of a Christian is: one who is completely fearless, continually cheerful, and constantly in trouble. This is exactly what this passage describes. God does not ask us to rejoice in the trouble, but in what the trouble does for us. He is not expecting us to screw up a smile on our face and go around saying, "Hallelujah, it hurts!" No, as the writer says,

For the moment all discipline seems painful rather than pleasant.
(Heb. 12:11).

But God is asking us to rejoice, nevertheless; not saying, "Hallelujah, it hurts," but "Hallelujah, it helps!" For, he points out,

Later it yields the peaceful fruit of righteousness to those who have been trained by it (v. 11). Notice that last part. It is possible to go through trials and never have them do a thing for you because you complain all the time. Trials never do anything for you if you are always grousing and griping.

Surely it is difficult to believe that God sends these things, yet the whole of Scripture is to this point. Perhaps you say, Satan sends them. No, God sends them, using Satan, perhaps, but you have never looked far enough if you look only at the immediate instrument. You must lift your eyes to the One behind it all and see that God sends these things. Therefore they come for our blessing and we are to rejoice in that.

Once in awhile in my reading I run across a passage that is so well put, so beautifully expressed, that it defies assimilation and I simply must quote it. I ran across such a passage in **Decision* magazine. It was an editorial titled "Hang Tough." It so captures the thought of this passage we are studying that I share it with you.

"So! Things are becoming a little rough and you want to quit. The pressure is too great, you say. No one appreciates your effort to spread the Gospel. The government has closed down your missionary bookstore, your hospital. Some religious bigot is inciting people to try to break up your meetings. People in the office are complaining about your Christian witness; they say your 'halo fits too tight.' Neighbors are beginning to look upon you as a nuisance. Someone wrote a letter in which he implied that your ideas were fanatical. Your family says you are old-fashioned and should stop 'forever going to that church.'

"So now you are ready to pull out, to cave in, to switch to something else. Enough is enough, you say.

"We, of course, do not know your circumstances, but we are going to throw away all the psychology books and offer a suggestion anyway. It is a rather crude Western expression: hang tough—like a ranch

---

**Decision* magazine, June, 1965. Used by permission.

hand-riding a steer. In the common coinage: don't give up!

"Things are going to be better for you. We know they will! Not because 'tomorrow is another day' or anything like that, but because God has promised it to His children. Read the promise in Isaiah 54:7,8. It may seem that it was written just for you. God never promised His children that dark days would not come; He promised that fulfillment would follow. Just as the angels came and ministered to our Lord after the temptation, so God will send His blessings to you. He will give you—Himself.

"Someday we believe you will see that the things you are now going through were necessary, in God's wisdom, to prepare you for what He has in store for you. You thought it was an attack on your integrity; God will give you a meaningful growth experience out of it. You do not have to try to make sense of life every minute, for God has already made sense of it.

"How foolish, then, to 'throw in the towel' right now. Did you imagine that the Christian life was to be all 'golden slippers in the golden streets'? What do you imagine the Bible is talking about when it speaks of 'overcomers'? You say you want 'out'—why? No courage? Are you afraid to face life?

"It may be that you will have to look squarely at certain things. As a parent, as a young person, as a church worker, as a human being, you have deliberately avoided a certain matter, taking the easy way out. All right, then, gird up your loins and go after it. The way to face the music is to face it! Don't stand there wilting and telling people you 'can't take the pressure.' Let God take it for you! That is why He is God. He is our strength and shield, the Bible says–a very present help in trouble.

"Remember, there is no such thing as weak-kneed Christianity. Christ builds strong knees–through prayer. You say you have had to take one setback after another; that at times it seems hidden forces are ranged against you; that life has played you a 'dirty trick.' But why should any of these things keep you from bobbing back? Look who is in front of you! *When the enemy shall come in like a flood, the Spirit of the Lord shall lift up a standard against him*[1] (Isa. 59:19).

"The Gospel has other words for other days, but the word today is, stay in there. Persevere. Show your mettle. 'Hang tough.' Strike a blow for Jesus Christ in spite of everything. For if you give in now, you may lose far more than you realize. But if you stick with it–and with God–there is everything to gain."

Now let us look at the second reason why trials come. They provide an opportunity to demonstrate our adequacy in Christ.

Therefore lift your drooping hands and strengthen your weak knees, and make straight paths for your feet, so that what is lame may not be put out of joint but rather be healed. Strive for peace with all men, and for the holiness without which no one will see the Lord. See to it that no one fail to obtain the grace of God; that no "root of bitterness" spring up and cause trouble, and by it the many become defiled; that no one be immoral or irreligious like Esau, who sold his birthright for a single meal. For you know that after-

ward, when he desired to inherit the blessing, he was rejected, for he found no chance to repent, though he sought it with tears.
(Heb. 12:12-17).

Here the writer summarizes the practical results of trials in our life: they make possible the demonstration of a new kind of living, which is what the world is looking for. The world is not at all impressed with Christians who stop doing something the world is doing. But they are tremendously impressed with Christians who have started living the kind of life the worldling cannot live. That stops them! And that is the life he is setting before us here.

First it starts with **correction.** *Lift your drooping hands and strengthen your weak knees, and make straight paths for your feet.* That is, if you keep on going the way you are going it will only get worse—that which is lame will be put out of joint. But stop it, he says, strengthen these things. Stop being so weak, stop being so anxious, so worried. How will the world get the impression that Christ is Victor if they look at you and you are always in defeat? Strengthen these things, he says, and learn how to live in peace with your neighbor, *strive for peace with all men.* And above all, *follow after or seek after the holiness without which no one will see the Lord.*

There is a verse that has bothered many. What does it mean? Do not forget that "holiness" is the exact Greek word that is also translated in this letter "sanctification." We saw before that "sanctify" means "to put to its proper use." When a man or woman is believing that Christ indwells him and gives him everything he needs for every minute, he is being "put to the proper use," the use for which God intended man. This is holiness, this sense of dependence upon and availability to God. This is what makes the world sit up and take notice as they see Christian men and women living the kind of life that is always adequate for every circumstance. That is the holiness without which no man can see the Lord.

The second phrase has to do with our **concern** for others. *See to it that no one fail to obtain the grace of God.* We are not to live our lives to ourselves. Others are looking to us and we have a responsibility to them. He points out the two things that will stop the grace of God in any man's life: bitterness and flippancy. *Do not let a root of bitterness spring up and cause trouble.* Bitterness is always wrong. No matter how justified the cause of bitterness may be, to have a bitter attitude as a Christian is always wrong, for resentment, envy and bitterness are always of the flesh. The trouble is, they are highly contagious diseases. If one person is bitter and continues in an unforgiving, bitter spirit, others are infected by this and it spreads and defiles many. This is the problem in many a church today. So if you see someone around you that has this problem, help them to see that this is a terrible thing that will wreck their life and destroy the grace of God, thus making it impossible to grow as a Christian.

The other thing that will arrest grace is flippancy, taking the things of the Spirit lightly as Esau did. He is the great example of this. Remember how Esau sold his birthright for a mess of pottage? He came in from the field hungry and saw Jacob cooking a mess of red lentils. When Esau saw the red lentils in the pot, he said to Jacob, "Give that red to this red" (pointing to his own red beard). That is one of the few puns recorded in Scripture. By that act he lost his birthright, not because he was an atrocious punster, but because he took the things of the Spirit lightly. The birthright had to do with the promise given to Abraham concerning the coming of a seed that would set man free from self. To despise it, as Esau did, is to say that the things that God offers to do for man are of no importance at all.

There is many a Christian, many a young person, who is in danger of despising his birthright, as Esau did, by saying, "I haven't time for these things, I'm too busy. I haven't time to concern myself with studying the Scriptures or walking with God." Unfortunately this causes a terrible reaction. As in the case of Esau, a hardness of heart sets in and when the moment of truth dawns it may be too late. When it says that Esau desired to inherit the blessing later but was rejected, *for he found no chance to repent, though he sought it with tears,* please do not misunderstand that. That does not mean that he tried to repent in his own heart but could not. The repentance he sought was not his own, but his father's. Repentance means a change of mind. When he came back to his father later and said, "Now, Father, I'd like to have my birthright," his father said, "It's too late, son. You sold it for a mess of pottage and it belongs to your brother." Esau wept bitterly and tried to change his father's mind, but his father could not change his mind; it was too late.

Here, then, is the ministry we are to have: to have

a life in ourselves that is characterized by a display of that holiness, that sanctification, that proper use of our humanity that makes God visible in us, and to manifest it in deep concern for the welfare of others, a concern that no one else miss the grace of God. That is the ministry, but what is the motive? For that we must look at the next passage.

For you have not come to what may be touched, a blazing fire, and darkness, and gloom, and a tempest, and the sound of a trumpet, and a voice whose words made the hearers entreat that no further messages be spoken to them. For they could not endure the order that was given, "If even a beast touches the mountain, it shall be stoned." Indeed, so terrifying was the sight that Moses said, "I tremble with fear." But you have come to Mount Zion and to the city of the living God, the heavenly Jerusalem, and to innumerable angels in festal gathering, and to the assembly of the firstborn who are enrolled in heaven, and to a judge who is God of all, and to the spirits of just men made perfect, and to Jesus, the mediator of a new covenant, and to the sprinkled blood that speaks more graciously than the blood of Abel.
(Heb. 12:18-24).

There is the motive. How can we carry on a ministry like this that has just been described? Not by being driven by fear. Not by the law with its demands upon us, "Do this, or else." Not by self-effort, not by the gritted teeth and the clenched fist and a determination that we are going to serve God. That will never do it; we have seen that throughout this letter. If we serve because we are afraid we will lose something from God, that frightens us as the law frightened Israel in the terrible scene on Mount Sinai. But it is not fear that is our motive; it is fulness; it is what God has given us.

You have come, he says, not to this Mount Sinai, but to Mount Zion, the place of grace; and to the new Jerusalem, *the city of the living God.* This is another term for the Kingdom of God, the kingdom of heaven. You have come under a new government, under new management. *And to . . . angels.* In the first of this letter we are told that angels are ministering spirits, sent forth to minister to those who are to be the heirs of salvation (in other words, Christians). Angels are here to help us when we need it. They are part of our resource. *And to the assembly of the firstborn who are enrolled in heaven.* This is the Church, those who are born in Christ, part of the firstborn of God, sharing His life with their names written in heaven, *and to the universal judge, to God who is judge of all men,* whether they are Christians or not. All men are on the same basis because they stand alike before God.

And to the spirits of just men made perfect. Who are these? They are the Old Testament saints we read about in chapter 11, men and women of God who lived in the days when the promise was given before the cross, who looked forward by faith and who are waiting now for us. *And to Jesus, the mediator of a new covenant,* the new arrangement for living. The mediator is not someone up in heaven somewhere, in some distant reach of space, He is the indwelling Christ. That is the point this letter makes. He is available to us. He is right here to be our strength, our righteousness, our wisdom, whatever we need. *And to the sprinkled blood that speaks more graciously than the blood of Abel.* When Abel's blood was shed it cried out for vengeance, as the book of Genesis tells us, but Jesus' blood does not speak of vengeance: it speaks of access, of invitation, of the fact there is no problem between man and God that is not settled by His blood. There is no longer any question of guilt. We can come completely accepted in the Beloved.

Thus, with all this on our side there is no need to fail, is there? That is the point he is making. Certainly it gets rough, certainly it gets discouraging, surely there are times when the pressures are intense, but have you reckoned on your resources? Have you forgotten them? I shall never forget a story of a Navajo Indian who periodically came off the reservation to see his banker. He was a rich old man, having made a lot of money in oil, and it was all in the bank. But he would come to his banker and say, "Money all gone. Sheep all dead. Cattle all stolen. Fences all down. Everything bad." His banker knew exactly what to do. He would go into the vault, put a lot of money into some bags and set it down in front of the old man. The Navajo would count the money, and his eyes would begin to gleam. Then he would come to the banker again and say, "Sheep all well. Cattle all back. Fences all up. Everything good." And out he would go. He was reckoning on his resources.

Now what he was counting on was a very flimsy security indeed, but the principle upon which he operated was right: he counted on that which was available to him. With the resources available to us there is no reason to fail. With all this working for us, who can be against us?

Finally, these trials come to us to mark out truth, the demarcation of truth.

See that you do not refuse him who is speaking. For if they did not escape when they refused him who warned them on earth, much less shall we escape if we reject him who warns from heaven. His voice then shook the earth; but now he has promised, "Yet once more I will shake not only the earth but also the heaven." This phrase, "Yet once more," indicates the removal of what is shaken, as of what has been made, in order that what cannot be shaken may remain. Therefore let us be grateful for receiving a kingdom that cannot be shaken, and thus let us offer to God acceptable worship, with reverence and awe; for our God is a consuming fire.
(Heb. 12:25-29).

This is the fifth and last great warning passage in this book, and it reminds us that these difficult times that we go through have a special purpose. Paul said in his letter to Timothy, *Perilous times shall come. For men shall be lovers of their own selves, covetous . . . trucebreakers,* and a long list of ugly things[1] (2 Tim. 3:1-3). These "perilous times" come in cycles throughout history, and they have a designed purpose. They are God's way of showing man what is passing and what is permanent. God is shaking the earth and the heaven. This is not the final great tribulation he is referring to, it is something going on right now. God is now shaking the earth and the heaven.

Have you noticed that the concepts on which man builds for security are being tested today as never before, and exposed as either true or false? Think of some of the things that men trust in. The security of number. We think if we can get enough people to join our club we will have strength. Today, alliances like that are collapsing on every side, agreements are merely scraps of paper, and no one can trust his associates very far. Then there is our trust in the power of organization itself. We think if we can get things systematically organized we can take care of all our problems. But now we are faced with the Frankensteinian monster of big government which is moving in to dominate more and more of life. It is well organized, but organization has run away with us and we are afraid of it now, with world government looming on the horizon. It frightens us, but it is simply a revelation of the weakness of our trust in the power of organization.

Take the common idea today of "the goodness of man." That was once heard on every side, but you do not hear it much anymore. More and more, as men are being shaken by what God is doing in the world today, we see violence increasing, and the indifference of man to his neighbor's need is demonstrated even here in the United States where we thought we were so civilized and cultured. There is our trust in the omnipotence of money. The older we grow the more we are sure that if we could get enough money things would be all right. We are being taught today to pray, "Our Father which art in Washington . . ." The result is that we are seeing more emptiness and meaninglessness and vacuity in life than we have ever seen before. Money, as our Lord reminded us, is never enough. This idea is being shaken so man can see what will remain. Our trust in the wisdom of science is threatening now the very destruction of the world in which we live, the whole human race. Not only from the atom and hydrogen bombs, but from such things as pesticides and other ways we influence nature. We are not smart enough to run our lives. That is what this passage makes clear.

Is it not rather revealing today that the most widespread description of our common reaction to life is, "We're all shook up"? God is shaking the things that can be shaken in order that the things that cannot be shaken may remain. The word to the Christian is, "Let us be grateful for receiving a kingdom that cannot be shaken . . . for our God is a consuming fire." God is light and God is love, and when you put those two together you get fire. Fire is both light and warmth. As someone has well pointed out, fire will destroy what it cannot purify, but it purifies what it cannot destroy. That is the whole explanation of life in this present hour. We are passing through the fire which is designed either to destroy that which can be destroyed, or to purify that which can never be destroyed. God is leading us through these trials and through the difficulties of our day, in order that we may learn to cry with old Job, back there in the oldest book of the Bible, *He knoweth the way that I take: when he hath tried me, I shall come forth as gold*[1] (Job 23:10). James Russell Lowell reminds us of the same truth in these words:

"Though the cause of evil prosper,
Yet the truth alone is strong.
Truth forever on the scaffold
Wrong forever on the throne.
Yet that scaffold sways the future
And behind the dim unknown
Standeth God behind the shadows
Keeping watch above his own."

"Our gracious Father, what a mighty revelation this is of the uncertainty of man's reasonings and man's abilities, but the sureness, the security that we have when we rest in that which can never be shaken. We are so grateful today, Lord, that by grace You have led us to this. We have tested it, we know it works. Now help us to stand strong, and 'hang tough' and to be Yours in every circumstance of life.
We pray in Your name,
Amen."

14

the intended life

The closing word of this letter is highly practical, crowded with many helpful things. This unknown writer (whom I strongly suspect to be the apostle Paul) felt very much like the sentiment of a limerick I often quote,

> "There was a young poet in Japan
> Whose poetry no one could scan.
> When told it was so,
> He replied, 'Yes, I know,
> But I try to get as many words in the last
> line as I can.' "
> (Anonymous)

And in this last chapter the writer has tried to squeeze in every bit he can in the way of practical application.

In this chapter, as throughout this whole letter, it is evident that God is not interested in religion. This may come as a surprise to many, but God is not primarily interested in religion but in life. He recognizes that life is lived in segments, like an orange, or in layers, like an onion. An individual has a social life, a business life, a sex life, a school life, etc. The Christian finds that, for him, life falls into two main categories: his contacts with the world, and his contacts with the body of Christ, the Church. His life, therefore, is divided between the world and the church. I do not mean by that a division in time, as Monday through Saturday for the world, and Sunday, alone, for the Church. I am talking about the relationship Christians must have with two kinds of people: the worldling and the believer. This letter closes with very helpful words about both. There is a section on life in the world, then one on life in the body, and then two magnificent verses on life lived at the center. Now let us take the first section on life in the world.

Let brotherly love continue. Do not neglect to show hospitality to strangers, for thereby some have entertained angels unawares. Remember those who are in prison, as though in prison with them; and those who are ill-treated, since you also are in the body. Let marriage be held in honor among all, and let the marriage bed be undefiled; for God will judge the immoral and adulterous. Keep your life free from love of money, and be content with what you have; for he has said, "I will never fail you nor forsake you." Hence we can confidently say, "The Lord is my helper, I will not be afraid; what can man do to me?"
(Heb. 13:1-6).

Here is a very striking commentary on Romans 12:2. *Do not be conformed to this world but be transformed by the renewal of your mind.* That is the Christian's calling: not to be conformed to the world but to be transformed in the midst of it. The Christian must live his life in touch with the world. There is a very dangerous and terrible philosophy which has been widespread among Christians (fortunately, it is beginning to fade), that Christians were intended to isolate themselves from the world, to draw lines of demarcation, to huddle behind high, towering walls that would exclude them from the activities, the thoughts, and the attitudes of the world. It is common today to meet Christians who have raised their children in a Christian atmosphere from the womb to the tomb, sending them to Christian schools, insisting they get a job in a Christian company, and thus living a secluded life for all their earthly career.

Now this is wrong. The New Testament clearly declares it is wrong. It is anti-Christian, and anti-scriptural, for it is against the command of God. The Lord Jesus has told us to be in the world and has sent us forth as sheep in the midst of wolves. Though we may be in a hostile environment, Christians are still expected to live in touch with the world. But they themselves are to be different. That is the point, that is the separation the Bible speaks of, *Come out from them, and be separate* (2 Cor. 6:17). It does not mean physical isolation but it means Christian attitudes in the midst of the world are to be different.

Now in this passage you have this difference outlined in a rather outstanding way. First of all, Christians are to have an open house to strangers. This is something the world knows little of. The worldling is content only to entertain his friends, perhaps a very limited circle. Christians are to entertain other Christians (that is part of what it means, *Let brotherly love continue*), but not to stop at this. *Do not neglect to show hospitality to strangers.* A Christian home is to be a center of hospitality to which strangers and worldlings are to have access.

Obviously this calls for initiative on the part of Christians. Strangers do not come around knocking at your door asking for an invitation to a meal. We must assume the initiative. Those strangers who come to church are a good place to begin, especially single persons, the lonely, and the aged.

This type of ministry has a special beneficiary effect upon the host as well, for the writer reminds us that *thereby some have entertained angels unawares.* Perhaps he is referring to the experience of Abraham, when three guests came to his home and he found that they were the Lord and two accompanying angels. At any rate he is indicating that surprising blessings can come from the entertainment of strangers in your home. Frequently you will find yourself more than amply rewarded by the initiative you have shown in this direction.

This is so practical I would like to pinpoint it with a question: Have you had a non-Christian into your home this past year? Have you taken this admonition practically and seriously and done this? For these things were intended to be practical means by which we can put into practice the tremendous themes we have been learning in the book of Hebrews. Well, that is the first thing, an open house to strangers.

The second relationship with the world must be an open heart to the oppressed.

Remember those who are in prison, as though in prison with them; and those who are ill-treated, since you also are in the body.

This means the Christian must not shut his eyes and ears to the needy around him. We must not be like the Levite and the Pharisee in the parable of the Good Samaritan, who out of a false sense of religious concern, shut their eyes to the need of the stranger and walked by on the other side, thus earning the rebuke implied by the Lord Jesus. Christians are to have eyes and ears and hearts open to those who are in need around them and do something about it. This is true whether the needy are in prison or otherwise oppressed or mistreated. As Christians, we are all called to the ministry of compassion.

I will not forget the shock that came to me while visiting in a home one day, to have a Christian woman tell me of an incident that had occurred the night before. Her neighbor had come to her in great distress of heart and asked for help in some temporary crisis that had struck her home. As this Christian woman told me about it, she said, "I don't know what I'm going to do. I moved here to get away from this kind of people, and if this woman keeps coming over to my house, I'll just have to find another home." My heart sank within me at that attitude. How totally unchristian!

Certainly this touches the delicate question today of civil rights. What about the black people, and the oppression under which many of them are undoubtedly living, not only in the South but in the

North as well? This verse should make very clear that it is wrong for Christians to ignore this kind of a question. We cannot defend all that is being done in this direction today, and perhaps some of the efforts to help are quite mistaken, but as individuals we must be responsive to the need.

Here is a point I would like to make crystal clear. I do not believe the New Testament gives the church warrant to issue proclamations on political problems the nation may be facing, or on social issues. As a body the church has no message to the world except the message of the gospel, the good news in Jesus Christ. But as individuals, the writer correctly points out, we cannot be rightly related to the God who loves all men everywhere and not show this in some definite, practical, helpful way. There must be deep concern about those who are oppressed, troubled, and underprivileged, and a readiness to involve ourselves in some kind of help.

Perhaps we need to open our eyes a good deal wider to these opportunities in our own community, and to see that there are those around us who need much help. A number of years ago I read an article by Averell Harriman. He was about to depart for France as the ambassador from the United States when someone said to him, "How is your French?" He said, "Oh, my French is excellent; all except the verbs!" Perhaps that is true of many Christians. We have such wonderful nouns, "Lord," "friend," "brother." And such inspiring adjectives, "noble," "sacred," and "divine." But sometimes our verbs are very weak–we have little action. But we are called to a readiness to apply in specific terms the love of

God by deeds of kindness and help to those who are oppressed around us. The Christian must have an open heart to the oppressed.

Then, third, he must have open eyes to the dangers of life, *Let marriage be held in honor among all, and let the marriage bed be undefiled; for God will judge the immoral and adulterous. Keep your life free from love of money, and be content with what you have* (Heb. 13:4,5).

Nonconformity to the world must certainly involve these areas. The loose sexual standards of our generation and the intense materialistic spirit of this age constitute a constant peril to our hearts, and we must beware of them. We must realize that God has undertaken to sustain the sacredness of marriage and that He unceasingly, unrelentingly judges violations of it. Therefore, we dare not heed the fine-sounding declarations being made today about a "new morality," as though we had passed beyond the ancient standards and they no longer had significance.

As this writer reminds us, God judges the immoral and adulterous. He does not mean that God looses lightning bolts from heaven against them, or that He causes terrible diseases to come upon them; these are not the forms of judgment. But we can see the judgment of God in the terrible tempest of mental pressures and crackups which sweep like a plague across this land. They are due to the breakdown of moral standards. The certain deterioration of life is the judgment of God when sex standards are violated. It is the brutalization of humanity, so men become like animals and live on the level of animals. This is so apparent in our day.

Then there is the danger of materialism. *Keep your life free from love of money, and be content with what you have* (v. 5). This means we must swim against the strong currents of a luxury-loving age. We must not give in to the pressures to "keep up with the Joneses," the mad rush to have all that the worldlings around us have. The weakness of the church is due in large part to the failure of Christians to be content with what God gives them.

This does not mean that all Christians should take a vow of poverty. There is nothing like that in the New Testament, for it is evident that God allows certain standards of living, certain levels of prosperity differing one from another. The point the writer makes is not that there is anything wrong in riches, but that we must learn to be content with what God has given. Contentment is not having what you want; it is wanting only what you have.

It is difficult to know where to draw the line between a proper increase in the standard of living, and needless luxury which is really waste, but the secret is given in the latter part of verse 5: *For he has said, "I will never fail you nor forsake you."*

That is the promise of God. He is our great unending resource and He will never fail us. Here is the strongest negative in the New Testament. The original carries the thought, "I will never, never, under any circumstances, ever leave you nor forsake you." It is a mighty declaration and on the basis of it the writer says we should declare, *The Lord is my helper, I will not be afraid* (of loss or poverty or anything else); *what can man do to me?* (v. 6). If I have God, what can man do to me? The point is that we must be content to take only what God gives us.

There is that wonderful story in Genesis concerning Abraham as he returned from battle with the five kings, having recovered the wealth of the cities of Sodom and Gomorrah which had been taken by the invading armies. Abraham brought this wealth back to the king of Sodom, who offered him a great reward. But Abraham said, *I have determined in my heart that the king of Sodom shall not be able to say, "I have made Abraham rich."* (See Gen. 14:21-24.) Abraham was saying in effect, "I will only take what God is content to give me. I don't want riches from any other source." If the Christian assumes that attitude he reasons, "If God grants me increase, fine; I'll take it. But I am not going to struggle after it. This is not my goal. I will not make the increase of money my purpose for living, for I am content with what I have." This kind of contentment permits us to be natural, uncritical. We do not go around judging those who have more than we have. We are quite content to let God deal with them, for we are content to have God deal with us.

Now that is the Christian in relationship to the world. Let us now look at life in the body. Here is life as a Christian must live it out in terms of his relationship to the body of Christ, the Church. Every Christian soon discovers that he is part of a new community–the community of the redeemed. It is a kind of secret society, the members of which are everywhere. Whenever you meet one you discover you share a relationship with him that is often closer than flesh and blood. You discover in experience the truth we sing of in the hymn . . .

"Like a mighty army
Moves the Church of God;
Brothers, we are treading
Where the saints have trod;
We are not divided,
All one body we,
One in hope and doctrine
One in charity."

That is true even though there are some who have suggested that by all appearances it should be revised to be sung something like this:

"Like a mighty turtle
Moves the Church of God;
Brothers, we are treading
Where we've always trod;
We are much divided,
Many bodies we,
Strong in hope and doctrine,
Weak in charity."

It is true there are many divisions outwardly in the body of Christ today, but there is also discoverable an inward relationship which links all true believers, who are born again and indwelt by the Holy Spirit, with one another. This is the life the writer now describes, life in that kind of a body.

The first thing we discover is that there is a structure of leadership within this body.

Remember your leaders, those who spoke to you the word of God; consider the outcome of their life, and

imitate their faith. Jesus Christ is the same yesterday and today and forever. . . . Obey your leaders and submit to them; for they are keeping watch over your souls, as men who will have to give account. Let them do this joyfully, and not sadly, for that would be of no advantage to you.
(Heb. 13:7,8,17).

The first injunction seems to look back to the heritage of the past, to those men and women who have died and left their testimony behind. Perhaps it refers to those who led them to Christ, whom they knew personally and who spoke to them the Word of God. He says of them, *Notice the way they ended their lives and imitate their faith,* and links with this the great declaration, *Jesus Christ is the same yesterday and today and forever.* What He was to the men and women of the past, He can be and is to us today, absolutely changeless. It is this changeless Christ which is the great refuge of the Christian in a changing world. Therefore as we look back to the men and women of the past, the Luthers, the Wesleys, the Moodys, or perhaps some godly Sunday School teacher or parent who has led us to Christ and established us in Christ, we are to imitate their faith which was fixed upon a changeless Christ.

This verse, by the way, is often misused today. There are those who say because Jesus Christ is the same yesterday, today and forever, He must inevitably do the same in every age that He has done in the past. For example, because Christ healed all those who came to Him, they insist all who come today must inevitably be healed. But remember this verse does not say Jesus Christ *does* the same, but that He *is* the same. His doing may change according to the times, but His character never changes; it is always the same.

Life in the body of Christ also involves a simplicity of belief.

Do not be led away by diverse and strange teachings; for it is well that the heart be strengthened by grace, not by foods, which have not benefited their adherents. We have an altar from which those who serve the tent have no right to eat. For the bodies of those animals whose blood is brought into the sanctuary by the high priest as a sacrifice for sin are burned outside the camp. So Jesus also suffered outside the gate in order to sanctify the people through his own blood.
(Heb. 13:9-12).

Here he warns against diverse and strange teachings which are linked, evidently, with food restrictions and external religious demands. These are the food faddists of the first century. It refers to those who insisted on Judaistic restrictions of diet as having spiritual value. This is seen in our own day the practices of some such as giving up meat for Lent, burning candles for certain observances, counting beads, or any form or ceremony upon which some religious value is placed.

Now let us be very frank and open about this. All through this letter the writer has told us again and again that such observances are simply empty shadows; they are pointing toward something, but the something they point toward is the real value, not the shadows. As he says here, *We have an altar from which those who serve the tent* (i.e., who indulge in shadow-acting) *have no right to eat.* You cannot have both the shadow and the substance; it is either one or the other. You cannot feed on the reality if you place value on the mere picture.

There is a very sly thrust here in these words, *which have not benefited their adherents.* He says, look at these people who have been so concerned about form, these lean, hungry, long-faced, haunted souls who want you to get involved in restrictions of diet and other outward forms. Look at them! They have not even been helped by their own programs; they are no better off for all their restrictions. Food does not strengthen the heart, he says, but grace does. Grace truly strengthens and if you try to feed your heart on empty religious ordinances then you cannot feed yourself upon the strength of God's grace! That is the whole thing. If you put value in the external, then the real can have no meaning to you.

This is illustrated in the Tabernacle, for back in the days when the sin offerings were brought into the Tabernacle the priests were forbidden to eat of them; the bodies of the sin offerings were taken outside the camp and burned there. The priest could eat of the meat of the burnt offerings, and the other offerings, but not the sin offering. Those bodies were cast outside the gate and then burned. Thus it was with the Lord Jesus when He came. They took Him outside the city of Jerusalem and put Him to death on a cross outside the gate. Thus the religion of the world, with its emphasis upon the external, is rejected by God. Man fulfills his proper function only by receiving what God has done in Christ, without any need for observances or candles or form or ceremony, but by a quiet act of faith. That is the simplicity of belief in Jesus Christ. It is so uncomplicated, so simple, so available to all.

There is also in the life in the body a sacrifice of service.

Therefore let us go forth to him outside the camp, bearing abuse for him. For here we have no lasting cry, but we seek the city which is to come. Through him then let us continually offer up a sacrifice of praise to God, that is, the fruit of lips that acknowledge his name. Do not neglect to do good and to share what you have, for such sacrifices are pleasing to God. . . . Pray for us, for we are sure that we have a clear conscience, desiring to act honorably in all things. I urge you the more earnestly to do this in order that I may be restored to you the sooner.
(Heb. 13:13-16,18,19).

There, again, is the practical side to this sacrifice of service which involves meekness. Let us go outside the camp, like Christ and, like Him, put up with misunderstanding and abuse and persecution from those who cannot see what we see in Him. Let us remember that meekness is the ability to take praise without conceit, and blame without resentment. This is the curriculum of grace, *Take my yoke upon you, and learn from me; for I am gentle and lowly in heart* (Matt. 11:29). Therefore let us go forth unto Him outside the camp, for here we have no lasting city, that is, nothing permanent.

Then there is a sacrifice of praise, "let us continually offer . . . praise to God." As Paul says to the Thessalonians, *In everything give thanks*[1] (1 Thess. 5:18). I have learned to gauge the spiritual life of a Christian by noting the absence or presence of a complaining spirit. When Christians complain they have obviously failed to grasp the great truth that everything has been sent for a purpose. Therefore, *in everything give thanks.* If all we can do is gripe, grumble, groan, moan and complain, it shows that we have failed to believe what God says is true.

The third aspect of this is sharing all things in common. *Do not neglect to do good and to share what you have.* The word is "communicate," or "to hold all things in common." That is not communism. Communism says, "What's yours is mine." But Christianity says, "What's mine is God's; therefore it's yours." There is the difference–a readiness to hold all things in common for the Lord's sake. Finally, there is a note on prayer. *Pray for us,* the apostle can say, *pray for us.* Every Christian needs enlightenment and empowerment. Life is too big for us to handle alone, too complicated, too highly structured. There are too many deceitful things about it. We are so confused, so easily bewildered. But prayer can cut through these illusions and bring us understanding and perspective. That is why the apostle continually asked, *Pray for us,* and the writer here says, *I urge you the most earnestly to do this in order that I may be restored to you.*

The final section is on life lived at the center.

Now may the God of peace who brought again from

the dead our Lord Jesus, the great shepherd of the sheep, by the blood of the eternal covenant, equip you with everything good that you may do his will, working in you that which is pleasing in his sight, through Jesus Christ; to whom be glory forever and ever. Amen (Heb. 13:20,21).

Man now possesses great nuclear submarines by which the oceans of the world can be traversed without ever coming to the surface. The secret of their tremendous power lies in a nuclear reactor hidden away in the depths of the submarine. That strange, remarkable force does not need any refueling but is constantly giving off energy, so the submarine never needs to go into port for refueling. So it is in the life of a Christian. In these two verses is revealed the nuclear reactor intended for every Christian.

Look at the elements of this: *Now may the God of peace.* In this letter we have seen what peace is. The nearest modern equivalent is "mental health." That is what you are after, is it not? In Christ we are in touch with the God of mental health, the God who intends life to be lived on a peaceful level. With Him is linked the Lord Jesus, the Great Shepherd of the sheep. I like that phrase, *the great shepherd of the sheep.* I came from Montana and know a good deal about sheep. If you are from the city you have probably learned about sheep from "Mary had a little lamb" and "Little Bo Peep." You think, therefore, that their fleece is as white as snow, and that if you leave them alone they'll come home, wagging their tails behind them. But I can assure you it is all a lie; it is not true!

Sheep are the most helpless of creatures. There are two outstanding characteristics of sheep: they have no wisdom, and they have no weapons. They are forever running off and getting lost and unable to find their way back, and if anything attacks them they are utterly helpless to defend themselves. That is why they need a shepherd. And that is why we need a shepherd, and why the Bible likens us to sheep. We have a Great Shepherd of the sheep. He is our resource, our provision–a God who is concerned about mental health, and a Great Shepherd who is there to watch us because we have no wisdom and we have no weapons for our defense.

Linked with them in this great process that is spoken of here is, *who brought again from the dead . . . by the blood of the eternal covenant.* There you have the cross and the Resurrection, and what these mean has been spelled out for us in this letter. The cross means the end of the old life of self-reliance, and the Resurrection sets forth the power of the new life, that marvelous inner force which is greater than any other force that the earth has known about. The mightiest demonstration of power the world has ever seen was not the hydrogen bomb, but the resurrection of Jesus Christ! The hydrogen bomb can do nothing but destroy.

The only power that earth knows anything about that can take life and put it together again is the resurrection power of a risen Christ. That is the power that is released within the Christian by the indwelling Christ within him. We talk about the conquest of outer space, but the greatest conquest ever made was when the Lord Jesus conquered inner space by moving into the heart of man, to plant within us the greatest power by which life can be lived—a power that heals and makes whole.

The result of all this is that God will equip you with everything good that you may do His will. This is the secret of effective service. You do not have to ask God to do this; He is there to do it, to equip you with everything good that you may do His will. There is no excuse for failure, is there? There is a full supply here and full ability, working in you. God is going to work through you, not apart from your will, but right along with it. You choose, you start out, but He is there to carry it through.

Then there is full acceptance, even before it happens, working in you that which is pleasing in his sight. You know you are going to please God, you know that you cannot help but please Him when you walk in this way and live on this basis. As Major Ian Thomas so accurately put it, "You are fighting a battle already won." But if we try to live in the self-effort of the flesh, we are fighting a battle already lost. Now notice this whole thing is wrapped around the most dynamic, most revolutionary, most life-changing phrase ever uttered by man, *through Jesus Christ; to whom be glory forever and ever. Amen.*

Through Jesus Christ. That is the secret of life, that is the way God intended man to live—through Jesus Christ. Paul can say, in Philippians, *I can do all things through Christ which strengtheneth me*[1] (Phil. 4:13). What an adequate program! What a mighty gospel! What good news for this present life! God intended it for you that you might live in your present circumstances, wherever you are.

The letter closes now with some personal greetings that are self-explanatory. They explain themselves.

"Our dear Father, thank You for this mighty letter coming to us across twenty centuries of time, reflecting the great truths that are still available, still demonstrable in our very midst. Help us to grasp and understand these, but more than that, give us the courage to step out upon them, to live life on this basis, that we might enter into the glorious liberty of the children of God,
for we pray in Your name,
Amen."